Etsy Marketing

How to Promote Your Business, Manage SEO and Maintain a Lifelong Store

Laura Smith

contained within this document, including, but not limited to, errors, omissions, or inaccuracies.

Table of Contents

Introduction

"A business has to be evolving, it has to be fun, and it has to exercise your creative interests."-Richard Branson

I'm Laura Smith, and I have been running a successful Etsy shop for nearly 10 years. Boy, what an adventure it has been! During the time spent on growing my business, I went through ups and downs. I faced challenges and overcame many. Some remain to this day, and I've yet to find ultimate answers. But, through my love for creating fresh products and product lines, networking on social media, and connecting with buyers, I learned quite a bit.

I have to admit something. Money drives me as much as it drives you. I'm not going to lie. I have a great product that I spend days, nights, and months developing. And I want to profit off of it. There's no shame in it. But, I also want to share a vision, bring in something unique and valuable into people's lives, and this is why I prefer Etsy.

You must be thinking: "But why Etsy? There are so many other platforms out there!"

Well, there's one specific reason I prefer Etsy over other platforms, and that is that I don't have to bargain for the value of my product. Etsy gathers buyers who appreciate value, history, authenticity, and quality, and are willing to invest in it. Unlike Amazon or eBay, they don't expect to shop dirt cheap. They come to Etsy each day willing to invest in what's important to them, and that's precious if you're a small business.

I used to be an Etsy startup, and I know how it feels to put so much work into your line without knowing if you'll ever even return your costs, let alone make a profit. And I know how it felt to see first sales coming in, and then plan around processing orders. Ultimately, my store grew so much that I had to hire staff. Can you believe it? Looking back though, I realized that there were many things I did that other store owners didn't, and there were also those I wish I did but hadn't. They would've made my work a lot easier.

I'm sharing this book with you out of my love for creating products and growing business like one grows a plant. I have to admit it: I'm a junkie for business planning, marketing planning, setting goals, and watching those goals fulfill. And I'm more than happy to share my knowledge with you.

I wrote this book for you to learn about what it takes to grow an Etsy shop after you've opened. As if establishing a product line wasn't as difficult enough, promoting your store is equally needed and demanding. But, it's also thrilling and rewarding, more than you could ever imagine!

With this book, I decided to start by explaining how small businesses benefit from Etsy. I feel like you need to know what makes Etsy a specific market so that you're able to steer your work and planning in the right direction because Etsy is no ordinary online shop. After that, I'll tell you all about Etsy shop SEO. Most store owners consider this part of the work a pain in the neck, but I love it. I'll talk about how you can emphasize the most important product feature to drive more organic traffic to your store and hopefully demystify that process.

Next, you'll learn how to discover and keep your consumer base. You see, every Etsy shop is unique. Each shop caters to certain personality types, age groups, shopping habits, etc. How these categories will look for your audience will largely depend on your product. I will help you find out how to identify and keep that target audience through audience research, targeting, and segmentation. This way, you'll know how to market your product to the right consumer profile. Aside from finding your ideal customers, you'll need to constantly promote your store to attract more buyers. You'll do this by continually promoting your shop. This book will also give you easy, reasonable steps to plan your advertising, from managing social media pages and ads to enticing consumers with freebies, giveaways, and discount coupons.

After that, I'll share my two cents on what you can do for your growth last. You see, we live in an ever-changing world. If one strategy would work time and time again, doing business will be much easier. But it isn't. As you get closer to the end of the book, you'll find out how to set attainable goals, track, adjust, and adapt to change to maintain business growth.

Last but not least, I'll advise on strategies you can use to find your best methods and practices. Etsy is all about uniqueness, and each shop will require a unique approach. I'll give you some ideas for finding solutions that fit your product and consumer base the best. At the end of the day, you probably chose that product category for a reason. You probably have a close understanding of its value, significance, and a group of consumers that benefit from it. This means that you'll have to adapt everything you read here to your unique concept. Feel free to test, explore, discard things and solutions that don't work, and discover what works for your unique shop.

Are you ready to start learning about how to market your Etsy shop? I'm as excited as you are! Don't forget to take notes while reading. You won't benefit from reading this book fast, but by analyzing how said things apply to your business. Take the time and pause wherever you feel necessary if it means that you'll write down your thoughts so that you can review them later. Good luck on your journey to growing on Etsy, and remember to stay authentic!

Chapter 1:

Just What Is an Etsy Store?

Etsy is an online marketplace. It connects buyers and sellers and revolves mainly around handmade and vintage products. Etsy will be a great marketplace if you're marketing arts and crafts, crafting supplies, houseware, paper goods, jewelry, small cosmetic brands, artisan foods, personal care, and clothes.

Figure 1

But, Etsy isn't only a place to sell arts and crafts. Planners, printables, designs, prints, and digital downloads, also have a place on Etsy. When it comes to selling vintage items, the platform requires that the items need to be at least 20 years old. You can sell vintage toys, books, games, houseware, accessories, jewelry, photos, clothing, and costumes.

While many things aren't simple about selling on Etsy, like designing, optimizing, and marketing your shop, the sales process is quite straightforward. The buyer will purchase a product from your listing, and you will receive an order and ship the item. Easy-peasy, right? If so, why so many Etsy shops fail, and why gaining customers is such a challenge?

Figure 2

How Small Businesses Use Etsy

Figure 3

Like any other store, whether online or brick-and-mortar, Etsy sales require regular work and attention. You will have to create well-optimized, compelling listings, and monitor sales to ensure all of your shipping is done timely and accurately. Good customer service is also important, considering the fierce competition and abundance of other small shops a buyer can go to if they're unsatisfied. There are many ways to benefit from Etsy as a small crafts business (Strine, 2011):

- **Targeted exposure.** Every store needs heavy advertising when they're just starting out. The good news is, by coming to Etsy, you're already accessing a pool of millions of customers who are likely to have an interest in your products. You don't have to go in and build your audience from scratch. It's enough to optimize your store and emphasize product types and categories. By doing this, the chances of interested buyers finding your store become much bigger.

- **Millennial-inclusive**. Millennials are everyone's favorite target audience. They're the most tech-savvy and prone to spending compared to other target groups. Their interests are diverse, and they enjoy getting out of their comfort zone to experiment with new products. Most millennials will gladly invest in multiple similar products from different brands to find the best option, unlike, for example, baby boomers who are much more cautious with their purchases. Every brand wants to cater to millennials due to their spending habits, but they're hard to reach. Luckily for you, hobbies and crafts are big interests among millennials. In fact, they make up for a majority of Etsy's customer base.

- **Easier sales and order management.** Who wouldn't want all of their orders neatly laid out, with funds already paid, and shipping addresses ready for fulfillment? I'd say every business owner would want that. Etsy makes it easier for you to charge customers and manage your orders, and it also helps schedule order processing and shipping.

- **Easy start.** Some might argue that gaining attention on Etsy is challenging due to competition, but let's be real. You are given a comprehensive platform to show your entire product line and have both free and paid advertising solutions available. On the 'free' side of things, if your shop is well-optimized, there are decent chances that they'll appear in searches, and paid advertising, when done properly, helps you gain loyal customers much faster than without online exposure.

However, there are also a couple of limitations to pay attention to when opening an Etsy shop:

- **Heavy competition.** On the one side, you're entering a marketplace with over 30 million consumers who enjoy arts and crafts. On the other hand, so are over 2 million other shops. It won't be easy to stand out among these competitive businesses. This is where authenticity comes into play. Etsy sellers have developed a signature esthetic over time, and similar products tend to *look* similar as well. Think well about how you can make your shop stand out from other similar shops.

- **Lack of website customization.** Etsy's search results can be confusing as they don't cohesively display results. Instead, you'll see a bunch of different products that contain the relevant keyword in their title. In that sense, it will be really hard to gain organic visits to your store before you gain positive reviews.

- **Lack of customer information.** Many shop owners complain about being unable to follow up with buyers because the website doesn't provide user information like their name, address, or email when the buyer shows interest in products. Instead, the necessary information is only made available for order processing. This means that you'll have to remind interested buyers to leave their email or phone number if they reach out for information, and make your other pages clearly visible and invite viewers to follow your social media or subscribe to your email list. Since this requires more action than usual, you'll build your list slower than if you were given tools and widgets for buyers to subscribe.

What You Need to Know Before Opening an Etsy Shop

If one could simply lay out rules for successful Etsy sales, there wouldn't be a need for this book in the first place. But things aren't so simple, are they? Main steps of successful Etsy sales include:

- **Planning and setting attainable goals**. Once you've established which products you want to sell on Etsy, you need an effective sales plan. Usually, the most effective step is to start with a single item category. You want to create that staple line for your store and products. One way to know which item category it should be is to review which products from your category are being sold most. Compare that list with your assortment, and you'll get a clear picture of which listing has the greatest chance of success. Here's how to plan and set attainable goals for your Etsy shop:
  - Plan by quarters

    Truth be told, chances are that it will pass between two and eight weeks before you make a sale, regardless of how great your product is. Arguably, it will take less time for customers to find your store if you already have an established online presence. But, if you don't, it will take longer. For this reason, planning monthly might prove futile. Instead, make your sales goals by quarterly milestones. For example, it's realistic that you can make 100 sales during the first three months, and then at least double the sales in the second quarter. Whichever number of sales you achieve during the first quarter, you can double up that number and set it as a second-quarter milestone. If you achieve the goal during the first six months—great! The chances are that you will reach over 200 sales in the first six months (given that you invested in advertising, social media, and of course, your product), and you can then pursue higher numbers. However, this calculation should depend on realistic chances of making a sale. It will be easier to sell 200 pieces of $10 products compared to $100. Keep that in mind, when setting your goal.

○ Plan your first sale

Many Etsy shop owners claim it took them weeks to make the first sale. However, that sale is important. Having any number of sales establishes your store as a legitimate, profitable business, and proves to other buyers that someone out there found your product to be great. If you notice that your shop isn't getting enough traffic to indicate pending sales, you can always ask your friends and family to check out your store. You only need a couple of five-star reviews for your products to be seen as marketable and worth buying.

○ Plan increasing sales.

Which strategies will be effective in increasing sales? Should you start a giveaway or an online competition? Should you up your paid advertising on Etsy and social media? Should you maybe send out some samples to online reviewers and influencers? Or, maybe turn to an already established complementary shop to see whether they'd want to participate in promoting each other's products?

○ Use the first eight weeks wisely.

There are many useful things you can do in the first couple of weeks while your sales haven't kicked off. Once you have a ton of orders coming in, it will be harder to take the time for creative work. So, while you still have the time:

- Plan your social media pages and posts. What will your pages look like? How often will you publish?
- Plan your content. What topic will your posts revolve around? Who will you target? Which messages will you try to share?
- Plan new products and product lines. What other products do you feel inspired to create? This is important because setting time aside to work new lines won't be easy with a ton of orders to process.
- Plan your advertising. Write your complete advertising plan, including a plan for each individual social media platform. This will spare a lot of time for future work when it will be a lot more difficult to fit planning into your daily schedule.

- **Registration**. Now comes a somewhat easier part of the process. Creating an Etsy account requires choosing a username, picture, a biography, and all the necessary setup fields. Don't forget to read the platform's terms of service and see how they reflect on your products and manner of sales. This is particularly important when managing customer service, refunds, and returns because these are the most common points of contemplation between buyers and sellers. Mismanage unhappy customers, and you risk not only losing your customer base from the start but also having buyers voice their dissatisfaction on other platforms, which could be damaging to your store's reputation.
- **Opening**. Now that you have your sales plan in motion, products ready to ship, and good knowledge of who to target, it's time to open your store. Once you've created the Etsy profile, hit 'Sell'' on the platform, and your shop will be open

for business. This part of the process really demands you to start treating your craftwork hobby like a business since you'll be choosing the name for your shop, the currency for selling your products, and of course, country and language.

If your consumer base is unlikely to know English, think well about how you'll present your store and listings. You should also design a logo for your brand or have a compelling photo, and you can set up a shop banner to have a well-rounded appearance of a well-standing manufacturer. These details may not have anything to do with the quality of your product, but the customers pay attention to all the signs of authenticity in the effort to avoid fraud or buying poor quality products. Keep that in mind, when deciding how to present your store.

- **Market research.** You have a store set up, and you have a product, or multiple types of products to market. This won't be enough to get your product to its ideal consumer speedily. Instead, you will have to optimize your store, which will demand using top SEO strategies to get your listing to behave in a search-friendly manner. What does this mean? In a sea of similar products, you want your product to show up in the search bar when a buyer is typing in the name of the product they want to buy.

- **SEO optimization and product listings (read more in Chapter 2).** This is where Etsy listings get tricky, as well as all other digital listings. In an effort to make your product more authentic, you most likely tailored a creative name for your line of products. A face cream named, for example, "Skin Candy," might appeal to your young female consumers, but will it appeal to search engines? Bear in mind, when the customer searches for a product, they do that based on keywords. These keywords and phrases reflect the type of product they're looking for and its purpose, main traits, and other relevant characteristics. For example, a buyer will type in "moisturizer normal skin organic" instead of "Skin Candy," of course, if they're not familiar with a brand. So, what do you do to make sure that your listing appears in relevant searches?

The answer lies in optimizing your entire listing. Like all digital platforms, Etsy requires you to fill in the relevant product information, including size, type, description, shipping, etc. But how they do that is relevant for you. The searches generate results based on keywords. It's important to keep that in mind when filling your listing. Each of the fields, from listing titles to tags and product descriptions, and even your store's biography, need relevant keywords. There's really not a lot of science behind this. Simply think about the type of information that's most relevant for the said field. Which information does the buyer need to see in that field to make it clear that this is a product they're looking for? Many sellers fall into the temptation of trying to use their listings as advertisements, so they waste precious space explaining the value of the product when they should be focusing on giving relevant information.

The second part of the optimization and keyword research process is to find out which are the most relevant keywords your buyers use when searching for your products. This is a highly individual matter which depends on the consumer base and the product itself. Aside from the product name and type, buyers often type in relevant characteristics of the products. The best way to find out which keywords are optimal for you to include in your listing is to simply look at other similar listings. Look at their tags, product descriptions, and prices to determine the right words and numbers for your product line.

- **Pricing**. Pricing is perhaps the most impactful part of marketing on Etsy. Prices of similar products can vary as little as a couple of dollars, but this optimization can make a great difference for both the buyer and the seller. First things first, analyze similar listings to discover which is the lowest and highest price for the product most similar to yours. This will give you an idea about how much prices vary. As a new store, you should aim to offer the best possible price, but it still needs to be sustainable for your business. Production and tax costs should be covered at the very least, or else you risk losing money instead of earning it on Etsy. After that, you should review similar listings to see which particular qualities affect the product's price. Is it the size, materials, or ingredients? Buyers often weigh the product's utility against its price and compare products to see which one offers more for a lower bargain.

This doesn't mean that the cheaper product will win, and this is where price meets SEO optimization. Remember, buyers don't know anything about your product unless you tell them. If you're marketing shaving cream, then that's all your product is to the buyer. But, if you highlight other important traits of the product, like how moisturizing it is, the practicability of the packaging, its ease of use, etc., the buyer will factor those benefits into the price. Many sellers forget to showcase all the product traits and benefits in their descriptions, so the buyer automatically associates the price with what they see on the picture, which is rarely ever enough for purchase. They need to know why the said price is justified. This is particularly important if you're selling quality hand-made products. Buyers can easily find cheaper alternatives unless they're reminded of eco-friendliness, sustainability, authenticity, uniqueness, or organic production. All of these details raise the value of the product in the buyer's eyes.

Figure 4

When you're researching similar listings on Etsy, keep in mind that the buyers will expect a similar price for a similar product and tolerate only small differences before choosing a cheaper alternative. Aside from this, price categories are also a relevant factor. A couple of dollars up or down could land your product into a completely different price category compared to other similar products, meaning it could easily be omitted from the search.

- **Creating stock.** Your listings should feature quality photos and appealing descriptions. Prices should set up to be competitive and cover your costs and shipping.
- **Selling.** You should monitor your account regularly and follow whether or not customers see and browse your products. The amount of traffic your listings get is indicative of whether or not buyers can find your products. If you don't seem to get the necessary amount of traffic, you should consider purchasing keyword specific ads to drive traffic to your listings.

- **Shipping**. Once you made a sale, shipping is another part of the process to think about. Buyers review and comment on how long it took to have the product shipped, how well it was packaged, the condition in which it arrived, and how much they paid for shipping. Buyers are usually happy with any shipping time that matches the disclosed information. Be realistic about your ability to ship products to buyers and give detailed, accurate information about shipping in your listings. If your buyers agree to a cheaper but longer form of shipping, they won't complain about it. It will bother them though if they pay extra for speedy shipping and the product arrives late, or if there's little information about shipping and the wait is long. It might be enticing to indicate fast shipping to drive sales, but if the claim isn't truthful, it will quickly backfire in the form of negative reviews or cancellations, and even refund requests. The main point with shipping is to offer what you're confident you can provide and disclose it fully and honestly.
- **Legality**. Finally, keep in mind to make your business legal. Etsy doesn't require a business license, but your local authorities might. You are solely responsible for the legality of your business and paying taxes, meaning you should make all the efforts to comply with legal requirements as if you were opening a physical store.

Costs of Opening an Etsy Shop

Etsy doesn't charge fees for opening an account or setting up your shop. However, you will be charged fees for sales and product listings. A 5% transaction fee is charged when you make a sale, and an individual listing will cost you $0.20. This is relevant when calculating the price of your product, which should also include any adjustments and personalization, and gift wrapping. US and Canadian sellers aren't charged fees for tax transactions (Goods, Services, and Harmonized Sales Tax), but sellers from other countries should include those costs into the transaction fee. Other services that might be charged with fees include:

- Processing fees for Etsy payments, which depend on your bank
- Advertising fees, including Etsy advertising fees that are calculated based on your daily budget and competitive listings
- Shipping fees that depend on the carrier plus add-ons like insurance and tracking
- Currency conversions, which you'll only pay if you charge different currency than the one registered in your account

Aside from the initial listing fee, Etsy will renew your listing after four months and charge a standard listing fee for the renewal. Listings are automatically renewed unless you cancel them. Etsy will provide you with a detailed monthly statement that shows all fees and deductions charged from your account. Keep in mind that funds need to be supplied to cover the costs of fees (which is why it is important to count them into the product price), or you're personally in charge of settling the fees within 15 days. If you account for all fees and costs when pricing your product, it's unlikely that you'll encounter any issues with charging fees.

Set up Your Etsy Store For Success

So, why are you better off showcasing your products in an Etsy store than any other platform or your brand website? First things first, Etsy has a reputation, and it already provides a customer base. Any other sales platform would require gathering consumers from scratch. On Etsy, there are already millions of customers waiting to try your products, given that you provide a high-quality product and handle marketing and advertising properly. Without a need for a physical store, your expenses are drastically reduced as well, and your products made available to a wider consumer base than your town.

Suppose you wanted to expand a physical store across multiple towns, an entire region, or multiple regions. In that case, you'd have to invest in storage, equipment, locations, staff, contractors, and advertising for each sales location. Etsy gives you worldwide exposure for free, or at a very low cost. Of course, there are many other platforms with a similar offering as Etsy, like Shopify, eBay, or Amazon. But, keep in mind that each platform offers different consumers, fee structures, listing designs, and sales models. Etsy is well-adjusted for small business and crafts and has an already built-in customer base geared towards particular product categories. Unlike other global marketplaces, Etsy is particularly geared towards customers who value creativity, quality, history, and tradition behind the product. Their design and layout are made to showcase these particular features, unlike other platforms that are uniform across all product categories and don't let your shop stand out.

Etsy's founders apparently had a good eye for the arts and crafts market, since the platform made $600 million in sales revenue in 2018 alone. Since opening, the platform gathered $2.1 million sellers, the majority of them being women (86%) who sell their products from home (95%). The numbers sound encouraging, don't they? But, if all of the stores were equally successful, the world would now have millions of female millionaires, which would be a fine scene. But it's not like that, is it? Many intricacies go into creating a successful shop, and your product's quality alone isn't enough to reel in consumers. Let's discuss a couple of particular details that make a difference to your store's exposure:

- **Store bio.** You can fill in this section with the usual basic brand information. This will be sufficient to show customers that your brand is reliable. But, more successful sellers talk about the reasons why they opened the Etsy shop, and things they're passionate about. This gives cumbersome bio information a tone, an emotional appeal, and makes your store memorable.

- **Store branding.** Much like with any other store, Etsy sales highly depend on establishing a reputable brand that appeals to its target audience. Branding means making your shop a unique one and knowing how to make it stand out from the bunch. It gives your store identity, values, and traits that buyers will want to relate with. Brand, by nature, involves creating an inspirational story about your business. The items you produce and the values you stand to affect how buyers will perceive your shop. When well-coordinated with your line of products, branding adds identity to the products and gives meaning to buyer-seller relationships. Branding makes buyers come in and check whether you listed new products, engage with your social media pages, and wait until you stock your products instead of buying from another brand. But, to achieve this, you need to create a unique **identity** around your brand. Branding is an important thing despite just having started with your store.
- **Brand identity** defines how customers perceive your shop and products. Your buyers will form an image of your brand either way, so it's best to start making conscious efforts to design how this image will look like. This is particularly important on Etsy, where authenticity drives the entire platform, it's sellers and buyers. Customers on Etsy come with an intention to make significant purchases and relationships with brands, unlike the majority of other platforms. Sales on Etsy demand brand identity to communicate your brand message and establish trust with customers. Etsy customers are already looking to develop a personal relationship with a brand, and all you need to do is give them a brand persona to relate to. But, how to create your brand's identity? Knowing which traits and values you want to communicate are necessary even before you list your first products. You'll find this out by answering the following questions:
    - What are your brand's values?

- How do you want your customer to feel when they're shopping and using your products?
- What's unique about your products?
- Who are your products for (what's your buyer persona)?
- What's unique about your shop that the customer won't find in any other shop?

Answers to these questions will affect your logo design, cover and banner photos, and your business name. These three main elements will create a brand identity for your Etsy shop. They are the main tools you will use to showcase your brand on Etsy and speak to your buyers. Let's discuss branding in more detail:

- **Shop name.** Craft a store name that is unique, memorable, and specific to your brand. This will help you stand out from competitors. Keep in mind that Etsy has some limitations for store names. You won't be able to use more than 20 characters, punctuation, or spaces. Additionally, each shop name bust is unique. Overall, the platform requires short, punchy names that will be easy to remember. Most users prefer switching spaces for capitalization, making different words in their name stand out while conforming to the platform's requirements (e.g., LaurasPantryJars).
- **Logo/Avatar.** Your shop owner profile will feature your personal photo, and the avatar is the place to upload your brand logo. Your shop logo needs to align with your brand and match all the criteria for brand identity. It needs to send the right message to the buyers and speak about your brand values. The choice of images and fonts determines how your brand will be perceived, and it can help distinguish between high-end and luxury and casual and affordable. Also, the logo should reflect the traits and features of your products. Describe your products in a couple of words, and you'll get a list of the

requirements for your store logo. Keep in mind that Etsy's avatar field is square-shaped, and if you deign any horizontal logos, they probably won't turn out well on the website.

- **Cover photo/Shop Banner.** The shop banner helps your store stay memorable, and it sets its tone, style, and mood. It is a visual representation of your brand values and identity. For this, you can use either a large cover photo or a smaller banner. I recommend using a cover photo because it's visible both from phones and computers, whereas the banner is only visible to customers who browse your store from their computers.

Great job! You now know how to set up a successful Etsy shop. But, this is only the beginning of your journey. If you created a quality product and poured your heart and all of your creativity into making something great for your customers, you should give it the best chances for success. How does one do that? Glad you asked. The next step on your journey is to optimize your store so that buyers have an easier time finding it. In the next chapter, we will talk about optimizing your Etsy shop for search engines. You'll find out what SEO is, and more importantly, why you don't have to pay an IT expert thousands of dollars and do it on your own instead.

Chapter 2:

SEO

Figure 5

In the previous chapter, you learned how to set up your store in a professional way. But that won't be enough to drive visits and sales. In this chapter, you'll learn more about using techniques to make your content stand out and reach your consumers a bit easier. These strategies are called SEO strategies. The following sections will show you how to use them correctly.

What is SEO?

Search Engine Optimization (SEO) is a strategy for increasing both the quality and quantity of your website traffic to rank better in organic search results (Adam, 2011). What does this mean? Your Etsy shop won't only rank on the platform's website. Much like social media profiles, Shopify, and Amazon profiles, it will appear in Google searches when a person types in a certain product or your shop's name. You want your shop to rank well both on the platform and when a customer searches for products similar to yours in search engines. These searches are called 'organic searches' because they're not affected by any other form of website advertising or linking (e.g., Etsy, Google, or social media ads, or a link/banner placement on other websites). To achieve high visibility on Etsy and in search engines, you will have to apply SEO strategies.

What Are SEO Strategies?

SEO strategies are a series of rules or recommendations to follow to help search engine algorithms recognize your website or your content as a relevant result for particular search queries. There's a lot of hype and mystery surrounding all-things-SEO because people have difficulty understanding what the process is. They think SEO optimization has secret hacks, and that the best practices are done by either splurging on advertising or hiring IT experts to install some mysterious codes into the website or content. But, this couldn't be further from the truth.

Figure 6

Imagine your website being a small book in a giant library that contains billions of similar books. If you were to make your book visible and help a reader find it, what would you have to do? Most likely, it would be some of the following things (Adam, 2011):

- **Make it stand out.** Authenticity and originality are the main requirements for any successful online installment. Not only can you get penalized for re-publishing already existing content (plagiarism), but you also need to make your book (store) stand out so that it's noticeable in the sea of others. A most logical way to do it would be to design your brand's identity and then align all of your online platforms representing it to that identity. This means incorporating brand identity and values into the design, content, titles, logos, and all other relevant elements.
- **Send a clear message-keyword optimization.** Clarity of online publishing, whether it's your store or relating website and social media profiles, requires sending clear, simple, understandable messages that both readers and algorithms

understand. Your content needs to contain and relate the most relevant keywords and key phrases for this to happen. Your store represents your products, and for people to find it, it needs to contain phrases and words they'd use when looking for particular products. Let's say you're a reader in a billion-book library, and you're looking for a book on renovating furniture. There might be great books out there, but unless they contain phrases "renovate furniture" or "DIY furniture renovation," you're unlikely to discover them. There might be some great, imaginative titles out there, but you don't have an entire day to browse. Similar goes for keywords. Readers rarely search past the first few pages of google search results or believe that the content of latter pages is of lower quality. The only way for your content to appear on those pages is for you to include words and phrases relevant to the searchers.

- **Be on good terms with the librarian.** Now, we get to explain how search engines work. If you were to showcase your book in a billion-book library, you would want the librarian to like you. If someone comes to them searching for a book, you want your book to be one of their recommendations. In the case of SEO, the Google algorithm is your librarian. It decides which are the best titles to present to the reader. But, here's the twist. Google's algorithm is not very smart. It's not a real, human librarian who can read your book and make their conclusions on its value to decide whether to recommend. If we were to compare Google algorithm's smarts to a human, it would rank somewhere with a primary grade-schooler. It can read, make associations, recognize how good content looks like, and place it among other content according to its evaluations. In a way, this not-so-smart tool is given a lot of power. And to persuade it into ranking your content high, you need to make the title, topic, relevant terms, and messages of your content clear. Search engine algorithms won't read your content in detail and evaluate its value. It will skim it and decide whether it is worth showing, much like you'd decide if a blog post is worth reading by scrolling through it first.

What Are The Three Key Elements of SEO?

Based on the previous example, you can see which details in your Etsy shop content need to be clear so that this child-librarian can conclude it's good quality, but also to have enough volume and substance to make a quality read:

- **Traffic/content quality.** These two are connected because you need to make your content appealing to the right reader. If your reader is looking for an organic face cream, they won't be happy to have a shampoo store in their search query results. Quality content means being on-topic and sharing relevant information.
- **Quantity.** Quantity of traffic refers to the number of people visiting your website—the more, the merrier, both in terms of visitor and content quantity. Your content will be popular if there are a lot of people looking for it, and if there's a lot of it to look for. Your website (store) will rank accordingly.
- **Organic searches.** Organic traffic is the one you didn't pay to get from search engines. The traffic comes from readers discovering your store/website on their own and browsing out of their interest. Organic traffic is most relevant when evaluating website ranking compared to other types of traffic.

How Does Search Engine Organization work?

Search engines are more than fields you fill in when looking for a website. The list of results you get is based on the engine's evaluation of the best quality content to show for a particular topic. If you have a question, search engines decide which websites answer them best. But how exactly do they do that? Our little allegory was merely an illustration of a more complex process. Indeed, no librarian is navigating the work of search engines, and it's most certainly not a child. In truth, search engines, including Google, use so-called 'crawlers' that obtain the information they find online. Crawlers come back with their findings and form an index, which is then pulled through an algorithm that matches reader queries with available data. A lot can be said on SEO and how it works, but for you, the following factors are most relevant:

Optimization

You must be wondering what optimization stands for and what it's all about. Optimization serves to help search engines understand what your content is about. When search engines know what your content is about, they'll know how to pair with it with the right readers or searches. There are many forms and methods for learning and using SEO. Mainly, SEO practices focus on titles and meta descriptions. But, there is far more to SEO than this. Applying SEO techniques to your site will help gain brand visibility.

Content

First things first, your website can't send its message without content. To optimize your content, you need to break it down into sections first, which will improve its readability. SEO-friendly copies have short paragraphs with a clear structure. Keywords are to be used in a natural way to fit the logical structure of the content but not overwhelm it. The so-called 'keyword stuffing' makes your content look fake and less believable. On the other hand, placing keywords where they logically belong has the exact effect you want.

On-Site SEO

On-site optimization includes website settings, like meta descriptions, tags, titles, subtitles, etc. All of these affect the readability and visibility of your website.

How Etsy SEO Works?

Your ideal SEO practices will depend on the purpose of the website. As an Etsy seller, your goal is to gain a high number of page visits, but also to generate purchases. If you want to generate a lot of sales, you'll have to have thousands of page visits daily.

Figure 7

Unlike what you may have thought, SEO isn't some groundbreaking solution to hack search engine rankings. Try to demystify the process in your mind the best you can, and start thinking about it as a series of minor adjustments to accommodate the demands of search engines and your visitors. These small changes can significantly impact traffic your store generates. For starters, SEO demands building user-specific websites and pages. Your options for that on Etsy are limited, but the limitation eases with the notion that the website already generates organic traffic, giving you access to millions of potential visitors. SEO is all about further adjusting your Etsy shop so that search engines can find and present it more easily. To understand how SEO works, let's first explain some of the essential terms:

- **Google index.** Stored information about your website. The content that Google stores in its index contain content and the URL of the page. When you say that Google indexed a certain number of your website pages, that means that it reached, read, and added the page to the index.
- **Crawl.** Crawling is Google's process of discovering new and updated pages. To do this, Google follows links, reads sitemaps, and consistently scours the web for new pages. Appropriate pages then get indexed. All this is done by the hands of an automated software called Crawler or Googlebot.

Proper SEO will also entail getting your site on the Google index. To check for this, you should enter your website name into your search engine. If the website doesn't appear in your searches, it could happen because it's newly launched, or the website design doesn't allow effective crawling. If Google receives an error when crawling, or your website is blocking it, it's also an obstacle to being indexed. There's nothing special you need to do for Google to include your website in its search results. This process is completely automatic.

Now, back to SEO. Often, people wonder whether or not they should hire an expert to optimize their website. There are arguments both for and against hiring an SEO expert. SEO experts are people who are trained to adjust websites for better search engine visibility. If not for the entire optimizing process, you can also hire an SEO expert to audit your pages periodically. However, this decision is both a matter of necessity and budget.

On the one hand, having a quality expert handle your SEO is a major time-saver, but can also be very expensive. On the other hand, poor-skilled experts can do more harm than good. With limited optimization abilities that come at the Etsy platform, paying for a service you can easily do on your own may come across as unnecessary. When it comes to Etsy specifically, there are several things that you can do to increase shop visibility. The first thing you need to remember is to frequently read and learn about best SEO practices since search engines change consistently. They regularly change term search techniques and criteria, meaning that some effective strategies now may not have a significant effect in the future. However, there are certain aspects of how you present your content and product that will most likely never change or won't change significantly. They mainly concern:

Product/ Content Quality

There are many elements that add quality to your Etsy shop. First, your product needs to be appealing, desirable, unique, well-produced, and overall high quality. From an SEO standpoint, however, you should look into features that distinguish your product from others. Other aspects that touch on the entire notion of quality include high-resolution images, well-written content, and a thoughtful shop presentation.

Keywords

A future where search engines don't care about keywords is extremely unlikely. Standards for optimizing keywords and the number of keywords to include in the content may vary, but they will always be relevant. In terms of selling on Etsy, keywords refer to words your customers use when searching for a product to shop. Keywords are also relevant for listing tags, which help buyers find your products in their searches.

Shop title and description

Your shop title must be unique, one-worded, and within 55 characters. These requirements might sound limiting, but they actually guarantee that no other shop on Etsy has the same name as yours, and there will be no confusion for the customers. It simply can't happen that they search for your store but get referred to another. This will also be your shop page's title and will be included in your shop's URL. Most new Etsy sellers are confused about their shop name when they first open the store, but worry not. You can change it whenever you want by editing in Shop Manager-Sales Channels. What to name your shop really depends on you. If you already have an online reputation and following, you can add your name to the title. However, it's recommended to add a brief description of the shop, items, your business name, and your personal name in your shop description.

Shop sections

Correctly naming your shop sections can help boost SEO because each of them comes with an individual landing page and a name that contains the section name. Visiting Shop Manager> Listings allows you to edit sections, which will affect their landing pages. The titles you create will then be visible in search engines, but they're limited to 24 characters. Each shop section should contain a brief description of your items. The best SEO practice for this is to use category styles, which are the easiest for customers to search and browse in your shop.

Listing pages

Item titles and descriptions are among the most important SEO elements for your shop. Your listing page will include a title of your item, and Etsy decides the length of the title, which will be displayed in search engines. Item titles should be clear and memorable and also based on customer searches. On the other hand, there should be something unique about it so that it stands out, meaning that the happy middle is to come up with listing titles based on customer searches and have a couple of unique words that are authentic to your brand.

Item descriptions are also important for SEO because they're used as meta descriptions in search engines. Use the first 160 characters wisely, because they will be displayed in search results below the page title. I recommend writing those first characters the same way you'd write a short social media ad, with the remaining text carefully written to appeal to the reader's needs without loud, flashy, in-your-face advertising. The first sentence of the description should contain a brief product description using primary, most likely search phrases and keywords.

Linking

Search engines like organic inbound linking. This means that you should have as many links as needed and natural for the content. It's recommended to include at least one link to your Etsy shop in your blog post, for example, but not to go overboard. Too many inbound links may trigger red flags for search engines and do more harm than good. At the very least, you should add a link to your Etsy shop to your website and social media pages. When it comes to linking specific pages from your store, do it as needed.

Why is Optimizing Your Etsy Shop Important

Just opening an Etsy shop appears like a lot of work, does it? As same as running any other shop, this venture will require consistent work on bringing in new customers. If you had a regular, physical shop, you'd also work on attracting customers consistently and diligently. You'd pay for newspaper ads, online advertisements, and you'd post flyers everywhere you can. When thinking about Etsy SEO, don't think about it as an unnecessary hustle. It is the same type of work you'd otherwise do when running a shop, only with a couple of advantages:

- **It's free.** You only need to learn about SEO to optimize your shop. You don't have to buy any services if you don't want to, except for perhaps having a photographer take professional pictures of your products, or a graphic designer makes nice-looking cover photos for your store. Other than that, all other work is under your control.

- **It takes less time.** You don't have to come back every day and re-optimize your shop. Instead, you can sit down periodically, once a month or every couple of months, learn what's new about Etsy SEO, and adjust your website (store).

- **It drives more customers.** SEO is almost like free advertising if done properly. Instead of having to reach out to customers, you simply adjust your store, so it's easily found. Depending on your market and store settings, whether it's local, regional, or global distribution, your pool of customers is much larger than with conventional shops, simply because anyone can find it if they browse or search for it.

SEO and Keywords: Optimize Your Listing For Best Performance

Figure 8

With that in mind, there are additional things that you can do to further optimize your store and listings:

- **Include product category in your product titles.** On the one hand, product names should be unique and creative to showcase authenticity and be memorable. On the other hand, you need to retain some familiarity and include necessary terms in the names of your products. Body lotion will be memorable if named: "Skin Crème Brule," but will a customer know what the product is for? Will it appear in the search results? What one should instead do is name the product something like: "Crème Brule Body Lotion for Dry/Oily Skin." This way, the title remains creative and interesting but still says what the product is and who it is for. It will be picked up by search engines much more easily, unlike the first option that could potentially end up in search results for desserts instead of skincare products.

- **Use long-tail keywords.** Long-tail keywords are sets of words or longer phrases that customers type in when looking for a product. Long-tail keywords contain three or more words (e.g., body lotion for dry/oily skin, from the previous example) that customers are most likely to type in when looking for a specific product. Long-tail keywords are important because searchers will most likely want to narrow down their search options to avoid having to go through hundreds of products they're not interested in. They reflect specific product characteristics that narrow down the search by type, use, who the product is intended for, and other relevant points. Etsy is specific for its product range, which mainly revolves arts and crafts, meaning that your long-tail keywords should focus on:
    - Sub-categories (e.g., Face cream: day/night, under-eye, etc.)
    - Use (everyday/daily, multipurpose, special occasion, etc.)
    - Product features (waterproof, organic, hand-made, herbal, recycled, etc.)
    - Materials (wood, cotton, canvas, porcelain, etc.)
    - Specialty features (unique, antique, luxury, etc.)

There are endless options for choosing long-tail keywords, so trying to learn all about them isn't the best use of your time. Instead, ask yourself: "what would my customer type in if they needed this type of product?" This will give you a very specific answer. Of course, there are many tools, and a lot of them free, that you can use to analyze popular long-tail keywords for particular searches. However, you should only use them if they match your product. This is important because customers who search based on long-tail phrases have a very specific idea in mind, and are most likely to buy compared to those who search shorter, more general phrases (an indicator of 'just browsing').

- **Prioritize keywords.** The order in which you add keywords is relevant for searches. First words should be the most likely ones, and the latter keywords should reflect further product specificity or customer need (e.g., for... [dry skin, brittle hair, etc.]). Primary keywords should take up the first 30 characters of the title, as those are most relevant from the SEO standpoint. You might be tempted to use the brand name first, but unless you already have a well-established, popular product line, chances are you'll need to pass on that idea.
- **Don't forget synonyms!** Customers use different terms when searching for similar products. Think about whether there are other similar phrases your product goes by, or slang specific to a customer base, and include it into your title. On top of that, make sure to also vary keywords across different products. This is important because Etsy won't let any seller monopolize the platform, so they only allow one or two products by a single seller to appear in search results. This is their way of making sure they're giving as equal opportunity for everyone as possible.
- **Don't forget the tags!** Product tags should always contain the main keywords. Those keywords should also consist of relevant search terms. This includes synonyms, product categories and subcategories, and all relevant terms associated with the product.

When thinking about keywords in general, perhaps the best way to go about them is through the process of brainstorming. First, write down your product name. Then, break it down into keywords. Look into those individual words and come up with terms that associate with the product. This process can go on and on, and you could easily end up with dozens of different and similar words and phrases. Now that you have this broad pool of short and long-tail keywords, you can simply go in and pick out the most relevant ones for a particular field. This will suit both search engine standards and limitations, and give you a simple, concise process to work with.

Bad SEO Practices: What Not to do When Optimizing Your Store

If you're new to Etsy and haven't published much online content so far, you might be tempted to do certain extra things to boost your store's SEO rankings. In this section, we'll go over bad SEO practices that might diminish your store's reputation among consumers, and earn a penalty from Google, or even Etsy. We wanted to discuss these practices because many of them can be found in blog posts that advise on SEO strategies, and there are even people out there who sell their services in using these unethical tricks. Without further ado, these are the things you should not be doing as a part of your SEO strategy:

- **Keyword stuffing.** It might be logical to cram as many keywords as possible across sections and fields of your store to drive traffic. But, this won't only be ineffective. Your store might be sanctioned by Etsy or penalized by Google. The use of keywords should never get in the way with content readability. If your text only consists of targeted keywords, it will be considered as keyword stuffing.
- **Misleading keywords/click-baiting.** The same way some recommend writing dozens of keywords into a product description to boost traffic, others might think that using misleading phrases in your title and description to spark interest is a good idea. It's not. If you're caught distributing misleading information on your store, you'll get sanctioned by Etsy, and probably lose any consumers you might have attracted.

- **Plagiarism**. You should never use other people's website content by copying and pasting into your fields and social media posts. Google will discover this and penalize you quickly, and Etsy could shut down your store overall. Create unique pieces of content for your products and social media pages. It will take time and effort, but it will pay off. Google has also updated its algorithm to recognize rewritten or spun content. These refer to practices of taking pieces of content from other websites and tricking plagiarism checkers by rewording the writing. When you do this, your content doesn't only become impossible to read, but you're doomed to ruin your store's reputation, aside from being penalized.

- **Advanced Black Hat techniques.** These techniques are unlikely to be used on Etsy anyway, as they require an administrator's access to a website. Still, you could come across unethical programmers who claim to be able to insert invisible text or cloak keywords into your shop fields to attract more traffic. Keep in mind that these techniques are prohibited across the web, and if anyone advises using them, it's very likely they're doing it to take advantage of you. They'll charge you for their time, and you will be the one facing penalties.

- **Link farming.** You might come across a recommendation to exchange links with other websites to promote each other. This might be advisable in moderation. For example, you can post links to your social media pages, or websites that appear relevant to your store. But, if you add dozens or hundreds of links to your website, and have those websites link back, it's considered unethical. By doing this, you're emulating the effect of having other websites link to yours due to quality and relevance, when it's not the case—only exchange links with relevant websites, and in moderate amounts.

Great job! You now know how to optimize your Etsy shop so that search engines pick it up more easily. SEO optimization increases the chances of connecting with the right buyers, and it's quite easy to do. As you learned, you need to prioritize the product's keywords, starting from the main category and subcategory, when writing titles and descriptions. You also need to make sure that other store sections and section names are written in a way that shows the most important pieces of information first, without much fluff. But, the work doesn't end here. The list of SEO practices banned by Google is ever increasing. In fact, some strategies, like keyword stuffing, used to be acceptable. All in all, if you do anything to mislead your consumers, or use tactics to trick search engines into sending you artificial, low-quality traffic (e.g., link farming), you could get penalized. In the next chapter, you'll learn how to find your target audience and connect with them to form a lasting buyer-seller relationship.

Chapter 3:

Finding (And Keeping) Your

Target Customers

Figure 9

Now that you know the best practices for optimizing your store for organic reach, what happens after you start reeling customers in? You then need to figure out how to keep them. If you know how to reach your ideal customer and have them come back for multiple purchases, you'll develop a loyal customer base. As months go by, you'll start noticing a steady stream of sales. These sales can be as little as a dozen, or as high as thousands each month. But, they are a sign that there is a specific group of people who adores your product and wants to enjoy it time and time again.

This loyal group of consumers then becomes your target customer base. In this chapter, you'll find out how to discover that loyal base so that you can start advertising to them and adjusting your listing so that it further expands and grows. If you follow instructions given in this chapter, you hopefully won't have to wait for long until you've developed that target consumer base. Instead, you'll be able to tell what and who to target with your product and advertising. Loyal consumers (those who'll stick with your brand) will stand coming in as soon as you launch a new product line. They could even start coming in right after you open your store (in case you haven't opened one yet). I'd advise taking notes while going through this chapter, as they'll give you a quite concise, step-by-step overview of what you need to do to establish and keep a loyal customer base.

Create an Ideal Customer Profile and Develop a Reader Persona

Figure 10

Finding and understanding your audience is important to know how to brand your products and also how to market and optimize your Etsy shop. Gathering information about your average consumer helps understand and access your market niche. The best way to do this is to perform audience research. Audience research helps you design your Etsy shop, and also adjust your ads, content, and messages. These elements, when done right, can increase your sales and help retain loyal consumers. But where to start?

Target audience is a consumer base you'll target with your marketing. These people are most likely to be interested in your offering. Your consumer base most likely has one or more things in common, whether it's demographic (age, gender, occupation, lifestyle), or certain behaviors and specificities that distinguish them from other people. The more specific you are with developing your target audience, the better. If you master the art of social media research, you'll have an easier time identifying a general target audience, its segments, and then adjusting your marketing to their characteristics. Targeting the right audience profile is important because it's impossible to shape content in a way that fits everyone's needs, style, and preference. If you aim to please everyone, there's a big chance you won't please anyone. But, how do you discover your ideal target audience? There's nothing complex about doing audience research. The process revolves around narrowing down your focus group so that you can expand brand reach. Here's how the process should look like (Strine, 2011):

1. Collect information about your current audience and customers

If your shop is new, you might have trouble with this part as you don't yet have an established consumer base. But, what you can do instead is look into the consumer base for products most similar to yours, and brands most similar to yours. What you need to do is get rough information about their dominant age (generation), geolocation (helps understand what the right geographic areas you should target are, as well as when to be online and schedule ads), language, and spending patterns and power. Gather the information about:

- Your consumer's budget,
- How much money they typically spend on products from your categories,
- How often they shop said products,
- How they choose to do it (e.g., whether it's online or from physical stores), and
- If they have particular financial constraints that limit their shopping ability.

Interests are also important when talking to your audience. You should look into what they like to do, watch, and read. For example, if your audience is into arts and crafts and likes to watch similar content, that says you can bond with them by sharing quotes and memes from popular shows for that niche. The same goes for books and hobbies.

For example, if your audience likes crafts, you can post inspiring DIY projects and perhaps talk about how they can be done with products from your store (if you run a craft supply store), or even do a project yourself and share the process, with linked products of course.

2. Discover Your Audience's Needs And Challenges (Pain Points)

Challenges, or pain points, are most relevant when it comes to branding, optimization, and marketing. You need to know how your product helps your consumer base solve a particular problem or fulfill a need. This can be applied across numerous niches. Skincare, for example, helps people care for their skin and resolve skin issues. Hardware helps obtain tools for creative projects and emergency repairs. Hobbies fulfill a need for beauty, creativity, and spontaneity, while fashion and vintage fulfill a need for adding value and meaning to one's daily life. All of this affects how you'll present your product.

3. Discover Audience Challenges And Life Stage

Next, you should think about your audience's life stage. Are they retired, parents, or still in college? This affects their interests, activities, and shopping capacities as well.

4. Read and Participate in Online Discussions

If you already have a customer base, you should follow up with what they chat about your brand on social media, forums, and other platforms. If not, participating in discussions relevant to your products can help establish yourself as a niche authority figure, and earn future consumers' trust. On the other hand, paying attention to what users say about your brand helps.

5. Monitor Keywords and Hashtags

Monitoring relevant keywords and hashtags is a good way to follow up with online trends and target audience activities. It can give you a great deal of information regarding your audiences' likes, dislikes, how they perceive and evaluate products they use, but also a great deal of information about their lifestyle. It can help you discover their interests, activities, problems, and challenges. Following hashtags and keywords also shows you what your audience finds important, interesting, funny, said, acceptable, or unacceptable. It can tell you a great deal about their social and political attitudes and values, which is important to incorporate in your promotional content. For example, an audience that vastly values liberty and equality may have a completely different taste for online content than the audience that values tradition. The first is geared towards growth, curiosity, questioning social trends, etc., while the latter values preservation of what they find important, whether it's family, culture, or both.

If you have predominantly one or the other group of people in your consumer base, it would be wise to look into your shop content and design and your social media platforms to see if it aligns with your consumers. On the other hand, if you discover that you have a diverse audience, then your job is to figure out what they have in common and focus on that while catering to different segments in different ways. Responding to findings of your social research can then be used to expand the target audience. Engaging with people of certain profiles and associating with their interests, as well as responding to their problems using your published content, product descriptions, and customer service, can greatly help in reeling in more similar people. Here's how you can use this information:

- Design social media posts using keywords, phrases, and hashtags you discovered
- Combine detected problems with keywords when writing product descriptions
- Design social media ads that use said keywords and phrases to appeal to the audience.

6. **Perform Social channel research**

Social channel research helps you discover the habits and behaviors of your audience regarding the use of social media. Discovering how your audience uses social media helps detect important pieces of information, like:

- What time they're online
- What type of content they engage with (like, share, comment)
- Which daily activities they like to post about
- What they shop
- How much they spend
- Etc.

You can take up a manual approach or use the software when doing social media research. The software can be useful to gather information quickly, but a manual approach helps you avoid processing an overwhelming amount of information, and instead focus only on the information you find most relevant. Remember, the software can only be adjusted to your needs to a certain degree. For example, research software will show you a long list of keywords, but you can only detect the context in which this information is used if you read and analyze the audience's posts and comments on your own. This is more complicated because it entails manually going through relevant pages and forums and writing down your observations, but it can yield more successful insights than those discovered through the software.

Manual social research will require you to follow posts, comments, and threads to detect indicators like keywords, hashtags, likes, preferences, needs, and influencers your audience follows. What does this process look like? First, you need to create a list of websites and pages most often visited by your target audience, and then discover places where they're most active. It can be your own pages, and likes and comments on your product images, but also other pages and platforms. Once you've created a list of most relevant places to research, you can create a table with the most relevant information for your brand, products, and advertising goals. You can then continue to read through posts and comments and write down important pieces of information as you discover them. At the very least, you should use already mentioned categories, but you can also expand your search to include other indicators that might feel relevant.

Social research can also help you discover the niche authorities that affect which products to use and how they're perceived. This is important because online personalities, whether website owners, bloggers, or social media influencers often affect, or even dictate, how the audience will perceive certain products. They also lead and dictate trends. If you discover which niche authorities your audience follows, you can then research those authorities and discover how to optimize advertising, content, and even your listings to cater to their standards and trends. Remember, these authority figures often have certain criteria to judge products, and you should discover and cater to these criteria. If your product doesn't align with niche trends, it can easily be seen as irrelevant.

More and more shop owners choose to advertise through social media influencers. They do this most often by sending free products for review, or paying for unbiased reviews if the influencer is too busy to do free reviews. It is up to you whether you wish to advertise in this way because it is a double-edged sword. Influencers who review for free are usually most impactful but have looked into dozens, and even hundreds of brands, and have exceptionally high standards. They will notice small inconsistencies and flaws in your products and compare them against the competition to see whether your offer is a worthy purchase. You need to be prepared for this kind of scrutiny if you choose to send out products for review. On the other hand, influencers who require payment for their work tend to give overall more favorable reviews but are not as influential.

7. Analyze Other Etsy Shops and Reviews

There are other ways to map out your target audience if you're still building one and stay up-to-date with the competition. You should create a list of major Etsy competitors, analyze how they shaped their content, and what their customers write in their reviews. Pay attention to what they like and dislike about products, and which words and phrases they use to express their opinions. Collect these phrases, and you've compiled the list of desired product traits and what customers don't like about the competitor's service. You can use this information to improve your listings and customer service, but also to tailor digital content.

8. Analyze competition

Competition analysis is crucial if you want to move ahead on Etsy. Whether you're a new store or looking to upgrade your current store, you need to know how to assume your place among competitors. For this, you'll need to evaluate their strengths and weaknesses. The first will tell you what you should strive towards, and the second what you should improve and avoid with your line of products and shop management and design. To collect this information, note the following competitor information:

- **How they brand their products.** Which approach was used to create a successful brand? Which values did they target? What was their inspiration regarding style and marketing? How they grouped/categorized their products? How did they choose to respond to consumer pain points and interests?

- **What are their advertising strategies?** Analyze competitor social media and their shop to find out how they designed their content, which makes their posts successful, and how they run their social media. How often do they publish posts? How did they design their ads? Which keywords did they use? What did they do to make their content and products appealing? Knowing this information will give you insight into competitor advertising strategies. While you should have your own, unique strategies, you should still model after the 'bare bones' of competitor strategies to conform with leading trends and consumer tendencies.

- **Which audience segments they reach?** This information will tell you exactly which audience profile will best respond to your audience, and what you should do to appeal to that demographic. This part of the process is quite easy. Read competition reviews and look into general information about their customers. How old are they? Which gender is predominant? What's their main location and social category? This general information gives you a clear direction to shape your target audience. Aside from that, look for particular sub-categories that stand out for different purchasing habits and product preferences. For example, senior consumers might prefer one product from the line, but the younger ones might prefer others. This will help you see which products to advertise to particular portions of your target audience, with previously mentioned tactics to shape content towards their needs and preferences.

- **What the audience likes and dislikes about their line of products?** Now, onto the next important thing. If you recall, we already talked about how product quality is an essential trait of every successful Etsy shop. Noting likes and dislikes is very simple. Pick a product to analyze and group reviews into two categories. Write positives and negatives on each side, and repeat the process for other most popular or remaining products. Those specific observations that stand out make for predominant product strengths versus weaknesses in the eyes of the consumers. What you'll gain here is a clear list of what to and what not to do with your product. Depending on the niche and individual product lines, consumers may have different pet peeves and favorites. However, this also gives you a clear picture of how to adjust your listings to provide what consumers typically like, and avoid those characteristics or features they dislike.

9. **Monitor Search Terms**

The audience talks about products in certain ways and using certain phrases. Make sure to include those words in your keyword base. Read through consumers' discussions and comments and note how they word what they're looking for, and how they describe the products they liked. Focus on sentences like: "I was looking for (keyword)", "I needed (keyword) to (keyword)," etc. Sentences like these give clear indicators of words and phrases to use to appeal to your consumer's needs and pains, and how to adjust your offering and advertising to what they like. Competitors have their advertising strategies, so look in and see how they use their audience's terms to shape their advertising content as well. So, what should you do with this information?

Discover how to make your product better, more accessible, and easier to use. Based on the information you gather, create an action plan for adjusting your listings, Etsy shop content (descriptions, titles, bio), social media pages (profile, posts), images, videos, and how you talk to consumers. This will help align better with their taste because you'll 'speak their language' away.

- Examine whether you can change your product to resolve challenges or meet goals better than the competition. Look both into things they do and don't do well, including their offering, policies, processes, products, social media, and content, and analyze what can be done better. Then, apply this knowledge to your store. For example, if the competitor chose to reduce product sizes so that they can sell at lower prices, think about whether or not there are better ways to compete with the price, like simplifying packaging or switching to more affordable suppliers. This way, you might be able to meet the competitor's price point while offering a larger quantity of the product, which will help rank better among consumers.
- Have a clear list of your product benefits and compare it against insights by the audience. In some of your earlier research, you noted strong sides and benefits of competitor products and their audience's likes and dislikes. Now, it's time to take this information and compare it against the competition. You can expect a similar response from the audience that the competitor got from their consumers. You can look into the main benefits of your products, and how they

otherwise rank among consumers. This will show which specific product features are most relevant to the audience, and which you should prioritize in your advertising and content.

- Use their vocabulary to express product benefits. You should use the list of perceived product benefits that your products contain to appeal to the audience better. Use the said benefits to tailor ads and social media in a way that's relatable to the audience.

- Think about how to give value through social media channels. Think about how you can help consumers overcome barriers in the purchase, either with a price reduction or shipping, adjust your listings and schedule posts to cater to their buying habits, and create the content they typically like to engage with.

Use Social Media: Instagram and Pinterest

Figure 11

Audience Segmentation and Social Media Reach

By now, you probably understand your consumer base well. You know what to offer, and how to write content in ways that showcase that offer the best way possible. So, what's next? If you look into your consumer demographic more closely, you'll notice certain traits or specificities that stand out in particular people. This is called audience segmentation and helps you notice consumer sub-categories.

Lookalike audiences

Lookalike audiences have major similarities with some differences when communicating with your brand. It is up to you to detect which are those. For example, members of your audience who prefer the same product may come from different age groups, or have similar behaviors according to demographics but prefer different products and content. Here's how you can use your knowledge of audience segments to cater to different audience sub-categories:

- Shape content towards different audience segments
- Structure and time ads and posts to cater to the right audience segments
- Adjust organic and paid social media strategies in content, captions, types of posts, and timing
- Redefine audiences regularly as they can change over time

Use Email Marketing to Keep Your Customers Informed

Email marketing on Etsy can be tricky because you're not allowed to use buyer's personal information for your own advertising purposes. Etsy forbids that practice, and customers hate it. The first thing I want to establish when talking about Etsy email marketing is that it needs to be asked for and easy to unsubscribe from. This is the first thing to remember before you even start contemplating how to build an email list for your Etsy shop. Never send an email to a customer if it's not through the Etsy platform unless they explicitly asked for it and have volunteered their email address. Now that we got that covered let's explain how one builds their email list from a platform that bans harvesting emails.

Before delving into building your Etsy customer email list, let's clarify that you're not allowed to email your Etsy customers and send them your signup link. You're also not allowed to pick up their email address and add them to your list, or email them based on that. What you are allowed to do is the following:

Advertise your email signup link in your store. For this, you can use your shop banner, shop description, product description, product images, etc.

- Include your signup link into your product. If you're selling downloadable products, you can always add your signup URL to the download materials. If you're delivering material products, you can print the URL on the packaging or include a card that contains it.
- Create an incentive and offer it in exchange for signing up. This can be applied across different practices, like starting a giveaway or offering a discount code for a signup. The philosophy behind this is to create a stock of free or discounted products and offer it in exchange for an email signup. Keep in mind to stay updated on Etsy's policies regarding emails, because it's always possible for their rules to change.

How to Set up Your Email List

Now, let's briefly layout how to set up your email list:

- Choose an ESP provider. ESP providers are online software platforms where you can set up your email to send, receive, and manage bulk digital mail. Without these, you'd probably have to send out messages manually, which would get your email blocked due to spam. Instead, sign up for an ESP provider, and you'll be instructed on how to create, manage, and distribute your email list.
- There are many ESP providers with different layouts, payment plans, and services out there. Etsy Pattern is one of the options you can use for your email list, since the platform has partnered with MailChimp, one of the providers, to give their sellers an opportunity to create a mail list. If you join this free program on Etsy, it will be easy to start building your list at no extra cost. However, this method was said to be only beginner-friendly, as it can't support larger email lists with multiple thousands, or even tens of thousands of users.

- Distribute your email list. Now, it's time to leave your email list URL wherever you can. It can be all over your Etsy shop, on your social media pages, and at the bottom of every social media post. If you have a good product and a good advertising strategy, subscribers will start coming in.

But, how to distribute your emails so that customers stay responsive, but don't get bored with them? While general recommendations state to email your list on a weekly basis, many established Etsy sellers only do that when they have an important announcement. Courtesy emails are said to bug subscribers and lead to unsubscribing, and being too quiet also makes them lose interest. What you should do instead is send an email when you have something relevant to announce or explain, like launching a new line, starting a giveaway, distributing coupon codes, etc. If you devotedly worked on your advertising, there should be something interesting to share at least twice a month. As long as your emails are genuine and truthful, but also relevant to the reader, your subscribers will want to read them.

Understand What You're Offering to Your Audience

Figure 12

Now that you know how to reach your target consumer, it's time to learn how to present your offer the right way. That's right! This section is all about developing a clear, cohesive understanding of your product's value and how to communicate it to your customers. Your product value is the foundation of your brand and business. Here's how to discover your core offer:

- What are the main features that the customer will benefit from?
- What is the feature they'll enjoy the most about your product?
- Who is most likely to benefit from this offering? If you've already done your target audience research, reflect on how the said features, or the core value of your product, will impact their life.

- What main pain points your product target? Have a clear image of consumer needs. By now, you probably have a clear idea of this, but it's important to identify core consumer needs that can be responded to using different product lines. Knowing specific pain points for each product line is important, but knowing these core problems to solve for your customers will help come up with unique, authentic products when you start to feel like it's time for a fresh launch.

Finally, it's important to always stay aware of what makes your business unique. What distinguishes your products from all others? What do you have that no other business has? If you're just looking for ways to introduce more authenticity to your offering, you can compare industry trends against what the competition is creating to see what's being neglected or hasn't yet been done. That way, you can gain insight into product features you can introduce into your line that no other business has. Having a clear value proposition will help you distinguish yourself from the competition, cater to specific needs, and remain memorable in the eye of the consumer. I hope you like this book so far! If you did, please take a couple of seconds to leave a brief review of the book and share your impressions!

Chapter 4:

Promoting Your Business (Without

Breaking the Bank)

Figure 13

If you've done previous steps correctly, you'll notice more and more traffic coming to your store, and orders will start coming in as well. But, there's something else you need to do for the growth to stay consistent. You need to actively promote your store. This chapter will show you multiple strategies that you can use to make your presence known and expose your brand to the audience. In this chapter, you'll learn about the right marketing strategies and promoting your shop on social media, and also about how to use paid advertising. You'll also learn about how you can use visual platforms like YouTube and Instagram to reach more audience and boost sales, and how to sponsor contests and giveaways to further engage with your audience. The number of ideas and recommendations you'll find in this chapter will be large, but you don't have to use all of them. You can focus on a couple of different strategies that seem to be most effective for your brand if you don't have the time or skills to practice all advertising strategies. The following sections will show you how to promote your store online, build your online reputation, and use word of mouth to gain more customers.

How to Effectively Promote Your Store On Social Media

After you've set up your Etsy shop and provided high-quality images of your products, it's time to start actively promoting your shop. It often appears as though good quality products sell themselves. If you've put in a lot of work into creating a quality product line and followed all the rules regarding SEO, you might think that the traffic will soon start coming your way. Sadly, this isn't true. With an abundance of online stores, on Etsy and all around, you'll have to take extra steps to gain visibility and exposure. Remember, you're competing with thousands of similar Etsy shops, and you need to find a way to stand out. So, how will you do that? The answer is by actively promoting your shop.

At first glance, marketing might sound complicated. It may appear as if you need complex data reports and statistics, certified experts to implement all the fine research studies into your strategy, and overall hundreds of thousands of dollars to fund all that. But that's not the case. With some learning and testing, you can promote your store effectively and see orders coming in like never before. One of the biggest values of doing your own marketing lies in the fact that you know your product inside out, and you also understand your consumer base much better than anyone coming from outside. This means that you should use these strengths to gain exposure for your store.

Create a Marketing Strategy

Figure 14

Your marketing strategy is about gathering all the amazing things you did to set up your store and using it methodically in a goal-oriented fashion. So, before you freak out about being unable to run a marketing campaign on your own, focus on thinking about it as just planning how you'll distribute promotional content to the right people to induce growth for your store. That's all there is to it! In this chapter, we'll review the exact steps you need to take to make your efforts worthwhile and develop an effective promotion strategy that will help your products find the way to the right customers.

You've already taken the first necessary steps, which were to title products in a true SEO fashion and model pages and descriptions towards your audience's tastes and preferences using keywords. What's next? If you did these steps properly, your products should appear in search results. Remember that product ratings and listing time also play a role in how the products will appear in search engines. This means that those products that have been on the market longer and have a proven track record are more likely to appear in searches than the fresh ones. This is why it's necessary to use both free and paid advertising strategies. These strategies will reel in new customers who will want to try your product even though it's new on the market (Blanchflower& Hodges, 2015):

- The first strategy to keep in mind is the **regular re-listing**. You should frequently re-list items. When you re-list an item, it will appear higher in search results, and then regress as new items are listed. You can automate this process by using the Renew tool, which will automatically re-list your products after a select time period. Each time this happens, your item will be bumped up in search engines. You will only be charged a small fee for this. However, make sure to monitor and adjust tags. Improperly tagged items can easily be missed out during relevant searches and shown for irrelevant searches, which is the last thing you want happening to your store.

- Another strategy you should try out on Etsy is signing up for **Promoted listings.** While you can promote your Etsy shop through different websites and panels, Etsy has its own advertising systems designed to give shops extra exposure. By signing up for a Promoted listing, you agree to pay each click your listing gets. In exchange, it will stay at the top of the search results. However, it will feature an 'ad' sign to indicate that the result is being promoted by the seller. On the other hand, the listing will be geared towards the target audience. Your consumers will be aware that the product is being advertised, but it will be a relevant product for them.

- Don't forget to **ask for reviews.** What's often problematic about reviewing products is that people don't like doing it, unless they're unhappy with the product and wish to share their frustration. While quality products on Etsy do get honest reviews, you should remind you satisfied customers to come in and leave a review. This will be important once your sales start to rise. The number of happy and unhappy customers will grow along with sales, meaning that you should motivate happy shoppers to share their insights. Positive reviews will enforce trust in your shop, and also help gain more exposure.

- **Branding**. We already talked about creating your brand and brand identity at the beginning of this book, so we won't further discuss it. But, it's important to note that branding is only one of the strategies that you can use to promote your Etsy shop, and not the only one.

- **Careful categorizing.** Make sure not to miscategorize your products. Your product descriptions should be short and on-point if you want the product to appear in relevant searches.

- **Social Media presence**. We already talked about creating social media profiles for your shop, but creating a social media presence and reputation is a whole other thing. It will require being active on social media and in relevant discussions to establish yourself as an authority for niche products. Your posts should also be carefully measured to be useful and answer important questions. This is important to remember because brands these days become too eager to be a part of the crowd, so CEOs use their social media as personal pages, and share casual details about their lives. Make sure to draw a clear line between professional and personal. And remember that your viewers are there because they benefit from your knowledge and expertise, not memes or videos of funny animals.

- **How-to's and Tutorials.** If you remember reading about YouTube in one of the previous chapters, now is the time to think about how you can further share your expertise through the platform to engage with the audience and profit. We already mentioned that you can post instructional videos about how your product could be used or inspirational project tutorials.

But, there's much more to YouTube than you might think. Much like Etsy, YouTube is also a platform with quite devoted niche audiences, and arts and crafts are big there. However, if you want your channel to grow and bring in significant advertising revenue, you'll need to up your game. A professional studio, proper lighting, tripod, camera, and weekly original creative videos are a good recipe to gain subscribers and views. Keep in mind that YouTube also offers paid advertising that can turn casual viewers into devoted subscribers. But here's the best part. YouTube is among the highest converting platforms out there. Influencers are said to receive over $50000 for their multi-million views only to do a 15-minute product review. YouTube subscribers trust their creators as they get to see the product performing and witness its quality. This means that if you manage to gain an audience on YouTube, you can expect your Etsy sales to increase drastically.

- When it comes to promoting your Etsy brand on **YouTube**, remember to add the link to your Etsy shop or specific products to your user profile, video description, and the video itself. YouTube is also a great place to advertise sales, discounts, new product launches, giveaways, and other incentives. Of course, a video description section is a great place to also add your mail list signup link, social media pages, and other relevant links.

- **Social media advertising.** Different social media platforms, including Facebook, Instagram, and Pinterest, have quite affordable advertising rates that average $0.20/click. This form of advertising is called CPC (Cost-per-click). Your ROI will depend on the effectiveness of your ads, so keep the following guidelines in mind:
    - Time your ads to when your audience is online

- ○ Choose an age group that's similar to your current customers
- ○ Choose target interests that relate to your product, or choose an audience that likes products similar to yours
- ○ Choose a wider reach to have a lower CPC price
- **Sponsor contests and giveaways.** There are numerous ideas for hosting giveaways and contests. You should choose a theme that's related to your product, and then ask for the audience to share a picture from your page on their profile, share one of your posts, or tag a friend into the comment section to enter. This will be a source of great exposure and boost the traffic of your store.

Launch Social Media Ads

Now, let's talk more about Etsy advertising. Considering that your Etsy store is digital, digital platforms will be most suitable for promoting it. Social media is one of the best tools for gaining consumers and exposure. Your store should have dedicated social media accounts, which will then be used for advertising. Facebook is a must for gaining exposure for your store, but Pinterest is also important. Pinterest is a different kind of platform compared to other social networks, and it mainly revolves around sharing images and creative ideas. In that sense, it's much more aligned with Etsy than other social media.

However, you shouldn't neglect to start a LinkedIn, Instagram, Twitter, and YouTube account for your store. Each of these networks is suitable for a particular type of content and can help gain exposure in different ways. For example, LinkedIn can help you connect with industry peers and establish your market reputation, while Twitter helps quickly share announcements and short promotional pieces of content. Instagram is more visual, and best suitable for posting nice images of your products and announcing launches, sales, giveaways. Finally, YouTube is a great place to showcase relevant and fun video materials. While the platform on its own can become a source of revenue income, it can also be great for posting videos that demonstrate how your product should be used, and creating other fun video content pieces that appeal to your demographic. Last but not least, each of these platforms has its form of paid advertising with quite decent targeting possibilities.

When setting up social media pages for your store, think about the type of content each is more successful with, and the demographic it caters to. This will help you plan and schedule content. You can do a quick google search for your niche and find out how your specific market works on each of the platforms, from the number of followers and popular hashtags to the best time to post and advertise, and even how to style your content to drive more traffic. To make your job easier, make sure to neatly log product images, descriptions, SEO elements (titles, keywords), and audience research. By the time you start working on your social media accounts, having all of the previous work organized and ready to use will help create content. Now, the time has come to start planning your content. On Etsy, your product is the point of focus. Regardless of any other content strategies, the image will be what attracts and maintains audience attention. This means that the time has come to discuss images in a bit more detail.

Post Eye-Catching Graphics

Etsy is mainly a visual place, and much more than other online sales platforms. It revolves around product authenticity, and any graphics you use must be high-quality to showcase that authenticity. Other than that, how you use graphics on social media is also highly relevant. You can find many online templates with customizable elements to adjust graphics for intended purposes. The frequency of your posts should depend on the niche and audience preferences, but it should be regular in any case. You should have a schedule for posting on different social media platforms in the hours where your audience is most likely to see the posts. You should plan according to your idea for how much interaction you want your posts to get, including likes, shares, and comments. You can compare your goal against online statistics, which will tell you what the best time for posting is. This time will depend on the type of posts, hashtags, and each individual niche.

Post Regularly On Social Media

Figure 15

There are many programs you can use to schedule your social media posts, including Hootsuite. This way, you can prepare your posts ahead of time and either let the software post automatically or just go in and review posts before putting them online. While it might be tempting to schedule a large number of posts at once, and have them launch all at the same time, think about your capacity to engage with all of them. You should monitor activity on each of your posts and be quick to respond to comments. Account for free time to monitor your accounts and discussions when posting on social media to leverage the maximum exposure you'll get, particularly if your posts are paid for.

Throw giveaways. Giveaways are a great opportunity to expand your reach beyond the existing audience. To organize a giveaway, you should plan incentives for participation and then think about the actions your viewers need to take to enter the giveaway. Usually, shop owners require following their social media or tagging friends into their comments. This way, your current products gain more exposure, and you gain plenty of future customers. Of course, each giveaway requires finding a winner. After you choose a winning account, you should send the prize to the winner. The winner will then be happy about their prize and post about it, which will mean extra exposure for your brand and social media pages. Giveaways require well-designed graphics that will be appealing to the audience.

Now, let's talk a bit more about creating social media ads. Ads are an important part of every advertising strategy. Your social media posts will reach those who like or have connected to your pages, but ads apply to all members of the targeted audience on each social media platform. Paid ads also allow you to target very specific audience traits, like age, interests, and consumer habits. Overall, whichever social media platform you choose, there's a bigger chance of upscaling your store with paid ads than if you're only counting on the organic audience.

Paid ads ensure that your posts appear in news feeds of selected social media accounts. Social media platforms allow you to fully customize ads, with the majority of them only dictating the ad layout. Other than that, you can set up the desired title, image, text, and the action button. How you design each of these elements will greatly determine how the audience will respond to the ad. Your choice of words and visuals should depend on your advertising goal and your audience. When designing your social media ads, it is also useful to return to your target audience research and look into their online preferences. Here, look for colors, fonts, and content styles they prefer. This will help you create an ad that the target audience will like.

Leverage Word of Mouth

Aside from using paid ads to gain exposure for your Etsy shop, you should also work on the method called 'word of mouth.' Having people spread the word about your store, products, and their experiences with them are as effective, if not more, as paid advertising. The majority of people (92%) believe the recommendations they get from their family and friends when shopping. This proves that word of mouth is quite a powerful form of advertising, that is, if you know how to use it properly. To get people to talk about your product, you need to be the one to advertise it first. Take every chance you get to talk about what you do, send out free samples to friends and family, or, for example, offer a small incentive if they bring in more people to check out your offer. Of course, you always need to work on the quality of your product. Your product must be truly great quality and useful if you want people to talk about it.

Great job! You now know about all the strategies that you can use to promote your store. If you follow the steps given in this chapter, you'll spend more and more time processing orders, and you'll get busier by the day. Once your store kicks off, your job will be to manage processes, monitor stock and shipping, and make sure that your customers are happy. But that's not all. In the next chapter, we'll talk a bit more about making your success last and keeping your brand's growth consistent. This is an important topic for many reasons. Many businesses start stagnating soon after a spike in sales, and their sales start to drop. Have you ever wondered why this happens? It is because they think they no longer need to try hard. They repeat the same routines over and over again, and their consumer base begins to narrow because new, more interesting offers start popping out. Before you know it, their shop is closed, and they have no idea what happened. I don't want this to happen to you. The next chapter will be all about creativity and learning how to make changes and adapt to new economic conditions, changing consumer habits, and new circumstances.

Chapter 5:

Making Your Success Last

Figure 16

If you did all the previous steps correctly, you should develop a functioning Etsy business with a growing consumer base. Your social media pages should be driving both organic and paid traffic, and that traffic should lead to more visits to your store and more sales. But, how to make this growth permanent? If it were so easy to establish and maintain a growing business, pretty much every hard-working business owner would find lifelong success. But it's not like that, is it? Staying devoted and continuously refining business and development plans, product lines, and advertising strategies remains a challenge for most CEOs. It's quite easy to start thinking that your growth rates will remain consistent, so the majority of business owners don't see a need for continuous work. This leads to stagnation, and eventually, a drop in sales and company growth. On the other hand, there are a minority of business owners who understand the need for constant growth.

Network With Other Etsy Sellers

Etsy supports teaming up with other sellers to support each other's brands. These types of collaborations are beneficial to everyone involved since each brand gets exposure to the new audience. It can be an affordable way for you to increase both traffic to your store and sales. Here are some ideas on how you can collaborate with other Etsy shops and brand owners to grow your brand (Adam, 2011; Strine, 20121):

- **Selling events.** Selling events can be a great opportunity to network, learn from other experienced sellers, and of course, engage a wider audience with your brand. Pop-up shops and craft fairs are some of the usual ways to team up with other sellers. In this case, the costs and work are divided, and you get to interact with wider audiences for only a portion of the costs when it comes to paying for events, organization, and catering, and of course digital resources like filming, web costs, equipment, and staff. You can also team up with complementary brands and create collections that complement one another, like fashion and accessories, or skincare and makeup. If you're selling arts and crafts, you can team up with designers, etc. This way, the products aren't competing with one another, but instead, making it easier for the customer to purchase all-in-one collections. You can add coupon codes, discounts, competitions, or giveaways to the offering for more engagement.

- **Group social media boards.** Joining groups of fellow Etsy creators can be done on Pinterest, Instagram, and Facebook to promote one another or promote as a team. You can share each other's links, review products, and recommend those that go well with your line. At the same time, each of the brands involved likely has loyal consumers who, when in need of a new product, will be more likely to support a brand from the group they trust, than purchase from an unfamiliar seller. It's recommended to group around a certain theme or style, which will make it easier to come up with cohesive graphics and posts that fit well with each brand. This way, you'll avoid collisions of different styles that might come across as over-the-top or appear competitive, making consumers feel like they have to choose or prefer one brand over the other. Making it clear how your products fit together and how the consumer benefits from all brands (e.g., skincare-makeup-fashion-accessories) help consumers think about all those brands first when deciding what to buy.

- **Loop giveaways.** Show your work in progress on Instagram and organize a group giveaway. These seemingly unrelated things do something really special. Showing how a group of creators makes their product demonstrates devotion and quality, and giveaways, of course, increase exposure. What happens here is that you get free advertising for all brands, and the first thing a consumer sees is how hard everyone involved works on creating products, which instills trust. That way, each new person who views group work is instantly presented with evidence of quality instead of having to go through that first phase of getting to know the brand. Keep in mind to review sweepstakes laws in your state or country to find out what you can and can't do when doing giveaways.

- **Share hashtags.** Hashtags are great tools for getting new customers. Come up with a creative hashtag that's consistent with the group theme, and use it when promoting group products. Hashtags are a great way to gain new followers, as everyone who looks at the hashtag can see all the posts with it.

- **Share resource costs.** You can hire photographers and graphic designers to create group visuals and split the costs. This way, you get quality work for your products at a lot less cost than if you hired artists on your own.

As you can see, you can benefit greatly from finding and supporting other Etsy sellers you like and whose brands complement yours.

Introduce Regular Changes and Updates

Figure 17

The economy is an ever-changing environment. Conditions change, markets change and transform, new products are constantly being launched, and, of course, consumers evolve and change when it comes to needs, tastes, and preferences. Your consumer base will develop different habits and patterns throughout the years. They might stop needing a whole line of products overall (e.g., vinyl records, floppy discs, Myspace profiles, etc.). You might have a profitable product now, but whether your product or service will remain relevant and needed largely depends on how you adjust and market your line.

As you can see, each ingredient in your success recipe grows, changes, and receives a new flavor year after year. If you want to stay relevant, you should constantly monitor and keep up with these changes. The good news is that there is one constant you can count on that links you to the market and prevents being pushed out, and it's your consumer base. If you work hard on developing a brand that caters to a particular demographic's likes and needs, they will stay receptive of any solutions you come up with for as long they're useful and relevant.

Let's say you produce furniture from recycled wood. While there's little chance that this industry will stop growing as it has just started to gain traction, it can always happen that other manufacturers come up with sustainable materials that make for quality, unique furnishings with the added benefit of having fresh, new, customizable items. What would you do in this situation? If you were smart and followed up with these changes, you'd know that there are a couple of ways to adjust. You'd alter your offering to cater to the same need (new, modern design, faster production), or switch to working with newly invented materials. Perhaps, you'd choose the former option as an immediate response to changing circumstances, and the latter as your transition goal. That way, you'd prevent losing your consumer base by going with the tide and acknowledging the need for a transformation. In this chapter, we'll dive deeper into how you can make your growth permanent.

Stay Focused on Your Niche

Focus on niche and vision. It's possible for one to grow tired of making a particular product line. To avoid this, discover what it is about your work that sparks passion and creativity. If your focus remains on the product, you'll last for as long as there's a need for that particular product. One way to prevent this is by mapping out the general vision, or an idea behind a product. To understand what your vision is, think about the following:

- What kind of solutions do you want to create?
- Why is this important to you?
- What vision do you wish to fulfill with your production?
- How your vision affects the world and society? Why is it important?
- What is it about producing the said solution that drives you to work hard and brings joy?

When you answer these seemingly vague questions, you'll have an understanding of the deeper meaning behind your work. For example, if you're producing organic skincare, perhaps there are motives to contribute to people's health and preservation of the environment, and mixing up herbs using apothecary tools brings you special joy and satisfaction. Here, you can spot a common thread. You help people look and feel better by 'cooking up' remedies in your home or lab. There's a large variety of tools and products that can be made using the said approach that serves the same purpose. So, if you ever grow tired of mixing up skincare, why not switch to food or supplements? Why not gain extra certifications and start producing herbal medicine? With this in mind, merely focusing on your current product line as the only thing you can and should work on seems to be limiting your potential, doesn't it? Seeing 'the big picture' of what you're passionate about opens up so many new possibilities. In terms of business, if you follow these passions and set out to plan long term (e.g., expanding from herbal skin care to herbal medicine), there will always be something that drives you. You'll always be up to something new, bigger, and better, based on the knowledge you gained so far. This will manifest in fresh, new products for loyal consumers to enjoy and shop, and of course, net profits for you.

Stay Original

Keep standing out. Etsy is a platform where you can expect new competitors to pop up daily, and existing competitors working to maintain their position. Make sure that your store is always well-optimized for searchers, appealing to customers visually, and that all of your platforms remain active and engaging. You need to stay active on social media and responsive on Etsy because customers take silence and absence as a sign that a brand is in some kind of trouble, or no longer operating. Always make your presence known! Maintain freshness and originality. A product can only be fresh and unique for a while. If you notice stagnation or decline in sales, know that the time for change has come. See what you can do to re-launch and improve your line, add beneficial properties, or make the shipping and use more convenient. Whatever you can do to put "New!" on your listings- do it!

Create Whole Lines

Keep your products related. Does the customer have everything they need to use your product? Will they need other products, tools, and supplies? Add additional products to your line if needed. Make sure to list and showcase as many side-products as you can for the consumer to easily pick up an entire set from your store. If they have to go to another store for extras, they're more likely to stay there if that seller provides what they need with less hustle.

Stay Competitive

Follow the competition. Your competitors are always after growth and improvement, much like yourself. If you fall behind major trends, there's a major risk from becoming irrelevant. The best way is to conform with major trends in a way that allows the uniqueness of your product to shine through. If trends revolve around creativity, add usefulness and sustainability. If they revolve around social awareness, add more diversity, for example. An easy way to do this is by looking into what your consumers lack to follow up with a trend, and add those characteristics to your brand and line. For example, eco-leather is trending, but many find the material to be less quality compared to real leather. This tells you that you can add unique product features that cater to the need for durability and resistance to wear and tear. This is a great strategy to move ahead of the competition by catering to the specific needs of your target consumers. It will add originality and specificity to your product that other products don't have.

Maintain Quality Visuals

Quality imagery and photos are the only things your consumer sees before buying. They need to create the same effect as picking up a product in a store, holding it in their hand, and exploring to find whether it's right for them. This tells you that the product images need to be:

- High resolution. You need to capture everything that's appealing about your product. Shine, texture, color, size, prints, shapes, curves, and everything a buyer would look for when looking at a product in a store needs to be visible in your pictures. For example, if the size of the product is one of its selling points, you should make the bottle/package sizing visible or place the product against another object as reference. These elements can be different from niche to niche, but they have one thing in common. High-quality images are necessary for sharp photos that give a detailed view of the product. Post a blurred image, and your buyer can no longer observe relevant details. There's no convincing them that the product has what you claim for it to have. With packaged goods, for example, you know that the customer will want to read the label and check out ingredients, benefits, effects, certifications, licenses, etc. If all of these aren't visible, it's highly unlikely that the buyer will believe your listing. It's advised to include 10 images per listing, all focusing on product selling points and benefits.

- Visually appealing. The color palette of your shop should be similar to those featured on the products, or complementary. This depends on your branding. However, color consistency across the design and layout of your store and social media pages and posts helps make a stronger visual impact and make products, and your brand memorable. Your images should please the eye, and be lit in natural light. Natural lighting enhances the image color palate and ads dimension, and organic feel if you may, while generic-looking photos appear less genuine and believable.
- Both up close and from afar. The former shows your product in detail, including shapes and textures, while the latter pictures can be used to showcase product context: its size, functioning, and proper use.

Develop a Routine

- **Have a routine.** Running your store will require the same amount of routine and devotion as if you were running a physical store. You should set up the following routines:
  - Product and store maintenance
  - Customer service
  - Creating products
  - Planning and updating advertising strategies
  - Reviewing and updating your company mission, vision, and values
  - Researching competition and consumers
  - Gaining equipment, knowledge, certifications, and qualifications needed for growth towards your vision

- **Balance out life and workload.** The same way passion and drive can keep you working at full capacity for a while, they can also cause a decline in inspiration and burnouts. First things first, make sure to find enough time to detach from your projects, unplug, and just do whatever makes you happy and fulfilled. Development plans, market research, and taking care of your store is rewarding and beautiful, but only up to a point. There isn't a final number of hours spent working on your business, and the work truly never ends. As soon as you solve one mystery, another idea will emerge. Count on that, and don't feel inclined to pursue everything that comes to your mind. In other words, know when to stop. Find your line between doing inspired work and neglecting your health, family, and personal life.
- A balanced routine is needed when managing **different areas of your business** as well. If you become consumed with planning, you can fail to take timely action. If you put a disproportionate amount of time, money, and energy into one aspect of doing business, other ones might suffer. Make sure to allocate your resources, both in terms of time, money, work, creativity, and staff equally across the board, or to the sufficient degree for the task at hand. That way, there won't be an overflow of work and resources into one area so much so that other areas are neglected.

Maintain Quality Customer Service

Don't forget the customer service! Develop highly engaging customer service, and make your consumers feel comfortable sharing their experience with your store and products. Do that, and your target consumer research becomes much easier. Consistent, direct feedback from consumers can greatly help when learning how to improve products and services, and follow up with leading trends. At the same time, it's important how you manage unhappy customers. Finding the line between accommodating their request and managing your resources is another important task to always work on. Making sure to improve customer experience by consistently listening to their feedback helps you optimize your store better, run your social media with more efficiency, and of course, update and improve products.

Customer Service Excellence Tips

Customer service excellence will get you far with Etsy shoppers and with trade in general. Many consider customer service as 'just' something they have to do to keep unhappy customers from sharing bad reviews on social media. But this isn't true. Once you develop your store and start processing hundreds and thousands of orders per month, some things are bound to go wrong. You should count on some customers having issues with their purchase, despite your best efforts to send out flaw-free packages to prevent damage. More than that, how you handle customer service can result in more positive reviews and repeat sales. Being there to answer questions and help out customers who have issues with their purchase instills trust. A customer will much rather buy from a seller who they can turn to if something goes wrong than the unresponsive one. Aside from that, they'll be more likely to stay loyal to sellers with whom they developed a close relationship than new ones.

Your customer service should be well-planned even before you launch products. Have a system planned out, include pre-written notes about how you'll answer some of the common questions. Your customers will often want to ask and get information regarding product certifications and use, your return and exchange policies, and shipping. Of course, if you need to sit down and write each answer, it could take a while. Instead, line out the most important pieces of information that customers might ask and then simply adjust it to their questions. Here are a couple more tips for quality customer service:

- **Be honest and open.** Never promise something you're not certain you'll be able to deliver. This particularly goes for product benefits and shipping, which are often a point of contempt between buyers and sellers. Don't oversell your product by stating it has features and effects it doesn't have. Instead of promising timely delivery, inform the customer about the amount of time needed to process and send out packages, letting them know which part of the process is under your control and which isn't. This way, your customers will have realistic expectations and won't be disappointed with their purchase.
- **Be detailed and transparent.** Everything related to your products, from photos and graphics, to titles and product descriptions, and of course, your policy, should be transparent and clear. Leave no room for doubt. Post images that show a realistic picture of your product with relevant features visible. Be clear and transparent about what the product provides, and openly state what you are and aren't willing to do with refunds and product replacements.
- **Fill out Shop policies.** Your Etsy store will have an entire section dedicated to sharing details about shipping, payment, exchanges and returns, and privacy. Use this section wisely to clear out and prevent any possible miscommunications.

How to Communicate With Customers

How you communicate with buyers can directly affect sales. Buyers will come to you to clear out any doubts before ordering a product, while the product is being shipped, or once it arrives and they have certain issues. They'll express certain concerns, and it is up to you to answer them properly if you want the customer to come back. Make sure that your tone is polite and welcoming. The customer shouldn't feel like they're bothering you. Give on-point answers and be honest and clear when giving out information. If the conversation starts to get unpleasant, copy and paste sections from your policy to explain that all of the asked information is a part of your general store policy, and not your unwillingness to cooperate with the customer. That being said, never set unrealistic expectations. Write your messages in a manner that shares information you possess and exclude personal opinions, assumptions, or any unaugmented conclusions from the discussion. If there are any repeated questions, you can add a Q&A section to your store description or shop policy. You can also set up saved replies for common questions or use auto-responses when you are away. This way, your customer won't be left without a response if you're on leave or taking a vacation.

How to Resolve Customer Service Issues

Customers may face many issues when shopping online in general, and of course, on Etsy. Production can get delayed, packages get lost, or they're not fully satisfied with their product. Whichever situation occurs, it is up to you to put out fires and resolve problematic situations to maintain the relationship with your buyer. Here are some tips for resolving issues with customer service:

- Express understanding. Whichever situation might be, make the customer feel heard by acknowledging that you understand how they feel.
- Be kind. Be polite and understanding with the customer regardless of their tone, anger, and frustration. Even if you feel like the customer is in the wrong, try to get to the bottom of the issue first and express interest in what they're trying to say.
- Find a win-win solution. Customers will often turn to you if their shipment gets lost and damaged, even if that's not your responsibility. Here, you need to think about whether or not you'll take a loss and satisfy the customer for the sake of keeping them loyal, or you'll be firm in maintaining your policy. Of course, this depends on the store, your product, offer, and

demand. Sellers can usually afford to take small losses for the sake of a good reputation if they've calculated their prices to account for possible losses.

At the end of the day, building a lasting relationship with a customer is more about communication and trust than anything else. Keep in mind that the customer doesn't have to have great communication skills, but you do. Communicating to resolve a conflict poses an additional challenge because it introduces negative emotions, both material and emotional loss, and possible misunderstandings due to the nature of electronic communication. Here are a couple of additional tips for building a great relationship with your customers:

- **Be proactive.** Don't wait for the customer to reach out before contacting them. Send a message to thank them for their purchase. Also, make sure to stay in touch and mail the customers about pending launches, competitions, important announcements, giveaways, etc.
- **Don't forget to keep up with window-shoppers as well.** If someone was interested enough in your product to send an email, but have never followed through with a purchase, you can thank them for their interest and let them know you're always there for them.
- **Be fast to respond.** It might be difficult once you start processing a ton of orders daily, but aim to follow up with customers within 24-48 hours. Let them know when their shipping is being sent when they can expect delivery, and of course, always thank them for reaching out.
- **Consider adding small tokens of attention.** 'Thank you' cards and cost-effective freebies, like small souvenirs, stickers, wrapping paper, etc., can be a great way to further advertise your shop and go that extra mile for the customer. These tokens of attention shouldn't take up a significant portion of the price but can be great for advertising your store. If the

customer wears a key chain or has a pen specially designed to reflect your store esthetic, it will be a lot easier to spark further customer interest and spread the word about your business.

- **Never place the blame.** Always speak in a neutral tone and address the situation, acknowledging how the customer feels, but don't blame anyone. Focus on things you can do to make things better for the customer instead.
- **Ask questions.** Buyers love when companies are interested in who they are, what they like, and their backgrounds. If they show interest in a particular item, you can ask to hear more about why they are interested in it, how they benefit from it, and what can be done to improve your line.
- Small things like **discounts for repeated purchases** or coupons and gifts for regular shoppers can contribute to repeated purchases.
- Finally, make sure that your **communication style and tone matches your brand**. How formal you'll be and what vocabulary you'll use should be in line with your brand values, and you can also the language of your customers so that they relate with your brand better.

Take Care of Your Resources

- **Protect your creative property.** Your unique product, images, and content need to be protected so that no one can replicate them without your permission. As soon as you complete your unique designs, have them registered as intellectual property.
- **Stay active on social media!** By now, you have learned a lot about using social media to engage with customers and run advertising campaigns. Keep in mind that social media remains as relevant for your business once you establish it as it was at

the beginning. Keep your social media posts and engagements plan, strategic, goal-oriented, and, more importantly, consumer-oriented.

- **Use up Etsy's resources.** Etsy offers quite a lot of support for store owners. They have detailed guide books revolving around relevant topics, they offer paid advertising, and they allow you to engage with other sellers to exchange tips and experiences. Don't forget to be active and connected with the platform the same way you're connected to your consumers. These connections help you learn from others' experiences, get educated, useful advice, but also establish yourself more firmly as a CEO.

Follow a Business Plan

Figure 18

Have a business plan. Creating a realistic business plan increases your chances of success and offers a comprehensive view of how you want to run your shop. A business plan is a document one creates to determine short and long-term goals, devise milestones, steps, and tasks to achieve them. A good business plan will help you solve daily dilemmas, schedule your work, and distribute your budget in the most effective ways. Creating a business plan is not as difficult as you think. In fact, you can write yours in less than 20 pages if you're just starting out. A business plan consists of a series of strategies one will use to develop their business. First things first, you need to define your product, its uniqueness, value, and place in the market, your target consumers, marketing strategies, and other relevant, more general guidelines for doing business. Here are the remaining key elements of every business plan:

- **Executive summary.** What's the big picture of your business? What are the end goals you wish to accomplish? Here, you should map out your shop's vision and why you think it's important.
- **Business description.** Describe your business and offers, and also how your offers fit into the current market. Think about:
    - How your products align with industry trends,
    - The company's legal structure, and
    - Previous work/industry experiences that will be beneficial to implementing the current business idea.

Define your general industry, main trends, and foreseeable future of the industry. Describe the type of business and whether or not it has a history.

- **Products and/or services.** Describe your product, its benefits, and its perceived value and utility for the market. Define your products and services, and list their unique traits compared to industry and competition: What makes your product stand out?
- **Marketing plan.** Lay out your target consumer base and your strategy for catering to that base. Explain how you'll develop your brand and build your reputation/establishment. Here, you'll need to define your consumer base, strategies to reach it, strategies and reasons for them to favor your products over the competition, communication strategies, and how you'll maintain customer loyalty and engagement.
- **Competitor analysis.** Layout the main strengths, weaknesses, and marketing strategies of your competitors.
- **Define main niche competitors,** how your work is different than theirs, which strategies you'll use when it comes to pricing and reeling in clients, and what you value and wish to apply to your business.

- **Operations/Management.** How will you structure your business? Which experts will you hire into your team? Which will be their roles? How will you distribute work? What will your production process look like? How will you secure successful operations?
- **Finances**. Calculate expenses, profits, and expectations. Define success indicators and account for financial growth. Also, define how you'll track the success of your shop.

Chapter 6:

How to Tell What Is and Isn't

Working for You

Figure 19

Finding your path and direction to follow won't be easy. There are endless options when it comes to making your business plan, designing your store, and marketing your products. The ultimate solution is to simply follow what proves to be effective for your business and abandon the strategies that prove to be ineffective.

Improve Your Business Constantly

You can take numerous steps to upscale your business, and they include (Malinak, 2012):

- **Plan around your uniqueness.** Center your brand around things that make you unique compared to others.
- **Focus on your niche.** The more time you spend catering to your consumers, the more you'll understand how your specific niche compares to others. This will help map out the consumer demographic to pursue, whether you aim to attract a broader demographic or strengthen the relationship with the existing one.
- **Persist and persevere.** In the previous chapter, we outlined the elements needed for creating a business plan. However, the very content of a business plan is highly individual and unpredictable in terms of success and efficiency. Simply put, coming up with success strategies doesn't mean that these strategies will work. You'll never be certain that your investment plan will see the desired return. You're best off making peace with learning by try and error. Since there's no guarantee of success, no matter how much you learn, research, and plan, accept that persistence and patience will be needed until you develop an intuition for the best way forward. The truth is that, despite extensive business and market studies, no one ever managed to list all the relevant factors that dictate one business's success, and no expert out there can tell you what you should do with full certainty. The best way forward is to learn, apply, adjust, and revise over and over again until you develop an intuition. "Rome wasn't built in a day," goes the old saying, and it's more than applicable to running an Etsy shop.

Give it time to grow, and take that time to learn, be creative, and try out different approaches.

- **Nurture passion and creativity.** The moment you notice that work is becoming cumbersome that means it's time for a change. That feeling of emptiness, loss of desire to create, and boredom, could easily be a sign that you're becoming stagnant. So, ask yourself if you've been engaging enough with your customers, have you listened to their feedback, and have you worked on applying that feedback? Keep in mind that the absence of improvement suggestions doesn't necessarily mean that you have a fully satisfied customer. It could mean a lack of engagement at their part. To have a fully satisfied consumer base is impossible. If you give them a great product, they'll have ideas about how to make it greater because there's no such thing as 'perfect.' Listen to that feedback, and see how it sparks your creativity. Even if there's no immediate need to apply improvements, you can always brainstorm ideas based on customer feedback and implement them when the time is right.

- **Acknowledge criticism.** Listening to people complaining when you're trying so hard to accommodate is never easy. But, it comes with the territory. As a CEO, you reap the biggest benefits of owning the shop and you're profiting the most. On the other hand, your team and consumers will see you as responsible for fixing everything that bothers them. From in-house management to customer service, you should always listen and acknowledge criticism, no matter how difficult it is. When critiquing, consumers tell you a lot about what can be improved about your product, and your staff tells you how you can improve your business. Arguably, you don't want to create a toxic work environment or fail to listen to what your team has to warn you about. This could have devastating consequences for your business. Likewise, if you fail to acknowledge customer complaints, they'll quite quickly find another brand that will listen to their concerns.

- **Follow the market.** Be always up-to-date with trends and market events. Compare your offer against that of the competition, and find out what you can do to improve.

Track Your Goals

There are a couple of simple steps that you can take to measure your sales goals regularly. Here are the right strategies:

- **Set goals based on the experience.** Don't start from the effect you wish to create, but by what's most likely to happen for your niche. Use the information gathered from competition research and audience research to set realistic goals.
- But, **account for the future.** Goals need to be growth-oriented. However, when predicting your goal, take advertising and other investments into account. Try to figure out how much growth you can expect from the extra effort you're putting in to promote your shop.
- Use the **SMART formula**. Smart goals are specific, measurable (you can quantify them), attainable, realistic, and trackable. Whenever you're formulating a goal, write down how you'll measure it specifically, how realistic and achievable it is for you, and which strategies you'll use to measure it. You should account for your resources and abilities when thinking about whether or not you'll be able to complete a goal.
- Be **on-trend**. Research your niche and track seasonal trends. Your customers will most likely expect special offers for holidays or discounts on particular days of the month. Also, make sure that your goals follow market fluctuations. If you

know that the sales speed up or slow down during certain times of the year, adjust your goals accordingly.

- Set **effort-based** instead of outcome-based goals. For example, set a goal to have a certain percentage of revenue increase instead of hitting an exact number of sales. Make sure to review and revise regularly to stay on top of your goals.

Here are a few extra tips for tracking your goals:

- **Visualize.** If you simply write down your goals and leave the note in a drawer, you will most likely forget about them. But, having a vision board and a planner that reminds you how much time to spend doing what, how many orders to process, or how many calls to make, assures that you'll stay on top of the goals daily.
- **Break down into manageable steps.** The best way to make sure that all of your goals will get an equal amount of attention is to break them down into yearly, monthly, quarterly, weekly, and daily. Having all of your goals expressed in daily actions to take will help keep a direction, and you'll also be able to check off the things you manage to do every day. Daily tasks and tracking will also help you identify if one or more goals are too difficult and you need to revise them.
- **Track based on performance criteria.** Focus on measuring how much you're doing some of the key things needed for growth. For example, how regular you are with social media posting, how many orders you process, etc.
- Also, **track the number of calls, sales, and meetings** you have weekly and monthly. This will help you spot rising and declining trends and react timely.
- Regularly **review sales**. Of course, many other things affect your business and should be observed, but sales are the main indicator of your growth. Analyze how all other goals, tasks, and steps affected your sales and earnings. This way, you'll

know what to expect and how to react when you see a downward trend.

Analyze Feedback and Take Action

Figure 20

There's an abundance of ways for you to collect customer feedback. The best thing about customer feedback is that you get all of the basic information you need to adjust the product to the market. Your customers will share everything they like and dislike about your store, including packaging, product quality and features, their experience with your shop, and their needs (pain-points). Most customers like to chat about what they like and need regarding a particular product category. Even if their statements don't directly relate to the product, they express everything that customers associate with your shop and offer, and you can think about further developing your product, or even creating new products, to meet those needs. But, to gain customer feedback, you'll need to take a proactive approach. Being proactive about customer feedback means taking the initiative and directly asking for their opinions on different matters. If you do this right, you'll gain a clear picture of where to take your business in terms of production and advertising. Here are the best techniques for getting customer feedback:

- **Surveys.** Customer surveys allow you to ask all sorts of questions and use different metrics to categorize responses. You can use shorter surveys on social media pages, or send out a longer survey monthly or by-monthly to gain a deeper insight into your customers' experiences. When sending out surveys, it's important to be economical and only ask questions that are relevant to your goals, open-ended, on-point, or unbiased.

- **Customer information.** You can also use emails and contact forms to allow customers to comment and leave their thoughts and opinions on particular topics. Or, you can simply create 'comment' and 'feedback' fields to let them write whatever they feel is important. You might miss out on important issues that make customers unhappy while pursuing goals that are relevant to you, which would be unfortunate. This way, by letting customers leave comments wherever they can, you're making sure that you won't miss out on any relevant issues.

- **Organize feedback and ideas.** Everyone involved with your business will have their idea for how your business can be improved. If you've done your job well, and now have consistent feedback coming in, organize these ideas in different categories and levels of relevance. For example, ideas and issues coming from a large number of either your employees or customers imply urgency, while an occasional interesting idea that doesn't seem to appear with the majority of customers and employees can be set aside for when you have more time to work on it.

- **Personalize responses.** If a customer reaches out with a concern or a suggestion, make sure that they receive personalized and not an automated response. You don't have to write the response yourself if you don't have the time. You can appoint someone from your management team to take up customer feedback, or even create an entire customer relations/service team.

Amazing! You made it until the end of your Etsy advertising manual! You now know all the essential steps to start growing and promoting your business and building a following. You know how to connect with customers, and also how to learn from their feedback. I want to leave you with a final piece of advice to truly value and celebrate your progress. If you started out small and made a first sale, that is huge! It means that your work is profitable. If you are marking supplemental or full-time income on Etsy, that means that you have a place in the market. You are a CEO, and that means something. Don't forget to celebrate each of your milestones and credit yourself for the success you worked for. I hope you enjoyed this book! If you liked it and found it useful, please take a couple of seconds to leave a review!

Conclusion

Congratulations! You now know the essential steps of promoting your Etsy shop. If the work still appears too complex, maybe this short overview helps to recall the basic steps. First, fill out your store profile fully and thoughtfully. Think about the necessary terms that best describe your products and business, and use them to fill out all the necessary fields as intended. Keep in mind to be short and on-point, because you can always go back and adjust your content once you learn more about your target audience.

Second, pay attention to search engine optimization. If you remember, I emphasized that there's nothing truly complex about SEO. It mainly revolves around highlighting and using keywords and phrases that are most relevant to describe the product and reflect words that the customer is most likely to type into the search bar while browsing. In that sense, the order and relevance of these keywords first focus on the main category and sub-category, best-intended purposes, benefits for the user, and then specific features that distinguish it from the other products. SEO is all about making your website (store) content easy for the reader to skim and search engines to 'crawl' so that they detect the key features. This way, search engines will understand what your content is all about and connect it with relevant searches. On the other hand, buyers will easily scan through your pages and quickly note important details about the products, which will grab their attention.

Third, you learned about the importance of actively promoting your store. You learned that the process begins with creating quality content (product and store descriptions), high-resolution photos and graphics, and then using that to craft compelling social media posts. But, before that, you must create profiles on relevant social media platforms, particularly Instagram and Pinterest. As you learned, Etsy is mainly a visual platform, and the biggest amount of traffic will come from viewers who find your images interesting. In that spirit, your next task is to go to social media, post relevant photos and unique descriptions of your products, and then plan your advertising. Now, it's time to layout your target consumer base and the ideal buyer persona you'll target. To do this, as you learned, you should research similar products and find out which consumer demographic is more likely to enjoy them. You also learned that you can rely on your intuition when deciding who is the best customer for your product, and how they benefit from it. Based on these findings, you can move ahead and write and schedule posts, competitions, giveaways, and discounts, in a way that's most suitable to your demographic.

You also learned that you should regularly engage in relevant discussions on your page and make your presence known. If you followed these steps, you most likely have plenty of knowledge to start paid advertising. You learned that social media platforms, Facebook, in particular, allow you to adjust the audience demographic in great detail, which is very important in terms of budgeting. You should begin by determining your advertising goals (e.g., how many likes, shares, and visits to your website URL) you want to achieve. Based on that goal, you can determine your advertising budget and the right audience to cater to. When it comes to the ad design, you learned that your images must be of the highest quality, and your ad text must be short, on-point, and engaging. Once you start running your advertising campaign, you can then analyze results by demographic and different platforms, and make adjustments to increase Return on Investment (ROI). Then, when it comes to advertising, you learned how important it is to build your email lists. Mailing lists allow you to continuously engage with existing customers for free, but it is a privilege you should use wisely. You learned that customers are quick to unsubscribe if you send irrelevant emails, so it would be best to contact them only when you have relevant news to share, or a discount or a giveaway to advertise.

Finally, you learned about what it takes to make your growth permanent and continuous. You learned that applying the same strategies over and over again won't work in the long run, because the market always changes, and customers always change. You learned that you should consistently update and perfect your website, social media, and your offer. To do this, you need to be up-to-date with leading trends and find out how you can conform to major shifts while still maintaining the uniqueness and authenticity of your product. That way, you'll keep your offer fresh and interesting. Embrace change, and get used to it.

Ultimately, you learned that you also need to embrace learning by trial and error. There are no specific rules for how each of the elements of your business and marketing plan should be laid out or how you should set your goals. It will take time for you to learn what works for your business and what doesn't work. After all, Etsy is quite a special marketplace. It is unique because it gathers people who care about quality first and foremost and don't necessarily go after the cheapest product. I want to leave you with a final message to follow your intuition and use all the creative juices you have. You have joined a special group of consumers who value originality and quality above all, so treating them like an average consumer won't be enough to keep their attention. Your Etsy customers are there because they look for the kind of authentic value they can't find in the nearest mall. They want their purchase to make a difference. They want to be a part of something bigger, something meaningful. Leverage that and follow the dream, a unique vision behind your product. That way, you'll always have enough creative ideas up your sleeve to remain relevant.

Discussion

Here are some extra Etsy marketing tips:

1. Serve customers like a pro. There's never too much time and effort spent making sure that your customers are happy. Quality customer service helps deepen relationships with customers and gain a direction for further business development.

2. List, Re-List, and List again. Customers love fresh products, and they always appreciate revamping standard lines and introducing improvements. On the plus side, new listings will always have a preference for Etsy search algorithms.

3. Be patient and persistent. It might take up to a year before you have a fully developed business. Don't rush to quit your day job, and instead spend extra time being creative and brainstorming new product lines. You won't have time for this once the orders start pouring in.

4. Photos and product descriptions! Remember that product photos and their descriptions make for the majority of your Etsy shop. Make sure they're polished, visually appealing, clear, and concise. Hire a photographer for the highest quality photos of your products because the investment will be worth it!

5. Don't limit advertising to Etsy. Use all legal and morally acceptable ways of promoting your store. At the very least, create social media accounts for your Etsy store and link them mutually. Share your social media links on Etsy, and add the link to your Etsy shop to your social media accounts.

6. Focus on creativity and quality. Quality and authenticity always come first. If you have to choose, choose to invest in

manufacturing a quality product over anything else. No advertising will compensate for poor customer reviews!

7. Post regularly. Have a schedule for your social media posts that is based on audience research for each platform. Research when your target group mainly uses a social platform in question and pre-write engaging. Quality posts.

8. Express product uniqueness. Every product out there is unique in a way, but not everyone markets that uniqueness well. Emphasize unique product features, and don't forget to include those details into your product titles and descriptions!

9. Always be professional! Study assertive communication and never lose your temper with employees, customers, or in online discussions. You might feel tempted to share a spicy comeback, but it will come at a cost.

10. Contact influencers. After you've done everything to produce a quality product and price it fairly, you can send out free samples to online reviewers. However, be prepared to get honest, but sometimes unfavorable reviews. Remember that influencers test out hundreds of products monthly and have high standards and expectations.

11. Invest in visuals. Whether it's graphics for your ads and cover photos or video expertise for video tutorials and advertisement, the effort will come back with a bonus. Graphics allow customers to check whether a product has said features, and if you manage to entice them with photos, you'll have no trouble getting them to buy!

12. Research your niche. Discover the industry, target demographics, and all other relevant traits of the people who will become your target audience. Also, research your competitors to see where you can improve your product and what you can do for your offer to be better than there.

13. Have a rich offer. You can start with a single quality product, but you'll have to further develop your offer to keep customers

entertained. Think about different age groups and personal tastes within your target audience, and create complementary lines with distinguishable features.

14. Always invest in quality. Whatever increases the quality of your product is worth the investment. Best practice examples include CEOs who live on minimum wage for years before affording luxuries because they're reinvesting in their business.

15. Educate all staff on customer service. Anyone on your team should be familiar with proper customer service. Even if they're not talking to customers directly, they may have to fill in for someone or help in online discussions. Every team member who knows how to communicate and put out fires is worth educating!

16. Advertise samples. Whether you're just launching your brand or starting a new line, free samples can help get more customers and increase sales. Also, plan out sending freebies with orders whenever you can to simulate buyers to shop frequently.

17. Be willing to invest! Quality work will require quality equipment, and growing your brand will require quality advertising. Don't hesitate to invest in paid advertising. It will pay off if your targeting is on-point, and you have a truly good product to offer.

18. Promote everything you do. Whether you renovated your studio or started working on a new line, share your journey with the audience. This brings you closer to them and also creates interest and excitement in trying out your brand.

19. Pretend your current customers are your only customers. Acting like customers are expendable won't go unnoticed, many CEOs think that they can do what works for their numbers and push products that are highly profitable for them, but this doesn't work. It's also very easy to spot, particularly in the era of social media.

20. Remember to network! Publish often on LinkedIn, engage in relevant discussions online, and share your opinion where you have something to contribute. Team up with other Etsy stores to either create products together or promote products like a group.

21. Maintain your integrity! Don't be willing to do anything for a profit, and don't try lowering product quality to maximize returns. Don't do unethical things for the sake of financial interests, because that never goes well.

22. Devote to your brand. Instead of focusing too much on your offer, think about your vision and the big picture of your brand. Think about how your brand fits into values you believe in, and how it benefits your community. Showcase these traits, and you'll always have fresh ideas, even if the interest in your staple product drops.

23. Devote to content excellence. You'll be doing quite a bit of writing if you're starting on Etsy. Your shop and product descriptions, social media posts, and blog posts won't require only creativity. They will require thoughtfulness and careful wording. If you don't have the time or skill to write quality content, hire a quality freelance writer to do it for you.

24. Share your work and progress. Keep a blog or a vlog channel, where you'll share your work experiences. Show yourself at work and combine the photos with inspirational quotes or useful tips. Whatever you choose to do, make sure you're putting out content that's useful to others.

25. Customize everything. Etsy shoppers appreciate all things unique and authentic. They won't like being treated like one in a million. They can go to the drugstore for that! Instead, aim to introduce authenticity and originality into everything you do.

26. Customize. Cater to as many people as you can. What better way to make your offer versatile than including customizations?

This is a great way to gain customers who would otherwise skip your product over a couple of details they didn't like.

27. Speed up shipping. We said more than once that honest shipping is satisfactory shipping. However you choose to distribute your product, buyers will be happy as long as the process goes as described. However, you should always strive towards providing speedy shipping and reducing the risk from packages arriving damaged. Be open to suggestions. Many established CEO's won't change their reliable routines, contractors, and service providers, so they miss the opportunity to improve their service overall.

28. Brand consistency. If you align all of the shop elements to your brand values, it will create a cohesive, memorable image of your store. Start from your brand vision and values, and use colors, shapes, and graphics that align with them. Account for customer tastes and preferences as well, and look into highly ranked competitor products to see how they catered to a similar demographic. Fit the elements that complement your concept into your product design, content, and visuals.

29. Be intuitive. You'll come across many advertising strategies, and you'll soon learn that one thing can be done in countless ways when it comes to promoting your store. Follow your gut feeling when you can't decide between two concepts or ideas. The chances are that you're on the same wavelength with your consumer base and that your likes and preferences also align with theirs.

30. Draw ideas from customers. When customers openly suggest or ask for a certain improvement or even a completely new product, do your best to deliver. If they were looking for a free solution, they'd be asking their friends and neighbors for recommendations. If they're reaching out to a business, they're ready to buy. So, give them what they want!

31. Don't launch products until you love them. The product is finished once you're in love with it. If there are still flaws to be corrected, or you notice a lack in certain product features, go back and improve it until you're happy with it. As an Etsy seller, you are the face of your brand. Customers will pay attention to whether or not you stand behind your product fully.

32. Accept imperfection. On the other hand, it's impossible to create something that can't be improved. Learn to tell when to stop polishing and adjusting, and how much time and effort is enough, whether it's shop optimization or product design.

33. Personality is all. Etsy shoppers look to feel special. They're willing to invest in handmade products and expect the entire shopping experience to be personalized. Whenever you can, have their package carefully wrapped with handwritten 'Thank You' cards—store owners who did this claim that it led to the massive sales increase.

34. Be realistic. You might be inspired by overnight success stories. But the chances are your store will take up to a year of devoted work to start bringing in supplemental income, and even longer to become a full-time job. Take your time with planning, and set your expectations lower to avoid losing your motivation before you even gave your store a decent shot.

References

Adam, T. (2011). *How to make money using Etsy: A guide to the online marketplace for crafts and handmade products.* John Wiley & Sons.

Strine, A., & Shoup, K. (2011). *Starting an Etsy business for dummies.* John Wiley & Sons.

Blanchflower, T. M., & Hodges, N. N. (2015). Understanding Etsy: social media and marketing within a community of sellers. In *Ideas in Marketing: Finding the New and Polishing the Old (pp. 818-821).* Springer, Cham.

Malinak, J. (2012). *Etsy-preneurship: Everything you need to know to turn your handmade hobby into a thriving business.* John Wiley & Sons.

All images sourced from https://pixabay.com/.

Figure 1: Ceramic Mug. From Pixabay, by Manfredrichter, (n.d.), https://pixabay.com/photos/ceramic-mug-ceramic-handmade-craft-4797733/

Figure 2: Knitting Handwork Hobby Handmade. From Pixabay, by Stevepb (n.d.), https://pixabay.com/photos/knitting-handwork-hobby-handmade-1614283/

Figure 3: Home Indoors Décor Design Creative Business. From Pixabay, by StockSnap (n.d.), https://pixabay.com/photos/home-indoors-decor-design-creative-2618511/

Figure 4: Art Boxes Colorful Container. From Pixabay, by Pexels (n.d.), https://pixabay.com/photos/art-boxes-color-colorful-colourful-1838414/

Figure 14: Email Newsletter Marketing Online. From Pixabay, by Ribkhan (n.d.), https://pixabay.com/illustrations/email-newsletter-marketing-online-3249062/

Figure 15: Shop Business Family Children. From Pixabay, by Geralt (n.d.), https://pixabay.com/illustrations/shop-business-family-children-1466324/

Figure 16: Money Coin Investment Business. From Pixabay, by Nattanan23 (n.d.), https://pixabay.com/photos/money-coin-investment-business-2724241/

Figure 17: Startup Start Up People. From Pixabay, by StartupStockPhotos (n.d.), https://pixabay.com/photos/startup-start-up-people-593341/

Figure 18:Analytics Computer Hiring Database. From Pixabay, by FotographieLink (n.d.), https://pixabay.com/photos/analytics-computer-hiring-database-2697949/

Figure 19: Coffee Success Arts Business. From Pixabay, by Feelphotoz (n.d.), https://pixabay.com/photos/coffee-success-arts-business-973903/

Figure 20: Illustrations Customer Experience Best Excellent. From Pixabay, by Mohamad Hassan (n.d.), https://pixabay.com/illustrations/customer-experience-best-excellent-3024488/

CPSIA information can be obtained
at www.ICGtesting.com
Printed in the USA
BVHW071225080421
604475BV00004B/472